Hospitality

Southern Style

A Collection of Treasured Southern Recipes
from Heirlooms by Radford
Lincolnton, Georgia

Compiled by

Carole Miller Radford
for
Heirlooms by Radford

ISBN 1-886300-01-1

First Printing - June, 1994
Second Printing - October, 1994
Third Printing - January, 1995
Fourth Printing - November, 1995
Fifth Printing - March, 1997

Printed in the USA by
WIMMER
The Wimmer Companies, Inc.
Memphis

The pineapple is the symbol which represents "hospitality" in the south and throughout the world.

The dictionary describes hospitable as "Behaving in a generous manner toward guests" and hospitality as "the spirit and practice of being hospitable".

My mother, Beatrice McCurry Miller and my Grandmother, Mattie Maude McCurry, epitomized both words.

My grandmother's farm in the red clay hills of Northeast Georgia and my mother's lovely ocean-front home in Charleston were the places where hospitality was taught to me and given to all who visited either place.

My Grandmother, called Nannie by her twelve children (seven girls and five boys), grandchildren and great-grandchildren always had enough food "on hand" for ten or twelve more people at any meal. She made her own butter, grew her vegetables, had cows, chickens and pigs. My early childhood memories are of her making her own soap as well. The smokehouse was filled with hams, sides of bacon and strings of peppers. The pantry was a dark secret place filled with a beautiful array of canned vegetables in glass jars and jewel-like jellies and preserves and, oh my, her biscuits and cornbread were glorious! She had a quick wit and an unmatched sense of humor. Everyone was welcome in her home at any time and for as long as they wanted to stay. She was almost self-sufficient and taught all twelve of her children how to use what they had and "make-do". In spite of being thrifty, she was outwardly generous, and kind.

My husband's mother, Grace Booker Radford, and her mother, Ethel Flowers Booker, were equally generous and hospitable, and they knew well the art of "making-do".

My Mother, called Nana by my children, entertained with the greatest of ease and could make even a brown paper bag a thing of beauty as could all her sisters and brothers. She was beautiful, gracious and very much a lady. One of the things my Mother did that will live forever in my memory was that whenever you visited her by yourself she'd bring a little tray with a flower in a bud vase and a glass of orange juice to your bedside. She'd sit on the bedside with you in the quiet sunrise over the ocean and talk about "things". What peaceful, special moments to remember. My sister, Betty Miller Wilkins, and I continue this tradition whenever we visit each other . . . a simple hospitable gesture, but how elegant and loved it makes one feel.

The cookbook contains recipes from Nannie and "the twelve" and other relatives and friends as well as many of my own which will help you practice "hospitality southern style" when you entertain your family and friends.

Carole Miller Radford

For other southern recipes and helpful hints see our cookbook titled ". . . hearts go home for the holidays".

Special thanks to the staff of Calico Kitchen Press, Hartwell, Georgia, for their help and friendship and to my husband, Buddy, and my family for their patience and support and for taste-testing many of the recipes.

This book is
dedicated with love
*to my granddaughter*
Beatrice Grace Ashmore
from her Nana

Table of Contents

PARTY TREATS & BEVERAGES

SOUPS, SALADS, DRESSINGS & PRESERVING

BREADS, GRITS, RICE AND PASTA

SIDE DISHES

POULTRY & SEAFOOD

BEEF & PORK

CAKES AND PIES

CANDIES, COOKIES & BROWNIES

DESSERTS

Party Treats
&
Beverages

AUNT JANIE'S CHEESE CRACKERS

1 C. butter, softened
8 oz. extra sharp Cheddar cheese,
    grated (room temperature)
1/4 tsp. salt
Dash cayenne pepper
2 C. unsifted all-purpose flour
Pecan halves (about 72)

Preheat oven to 350°. In a large mixing bowl, combine butter, cheese, salt and pepper. Mix well until blended (using your hands mixes it best). Add the flour a little at a time. When dough is smooth, flour the palms of your hands and roll dough into walnut-size pieces. Place on ungreased cookie sheets about 1" apart. Place a pecan into the center of each and press down. Bake for 20 minutes. Do not overcook. Store in airtight container. Makes 6 dozen.

Janie McCurry
Atlanta/Sparta, GA

CHEESE PUFFS

2 1/2 C. self-rising flour
2 sticks margarine
2 C. grated sharp cheese
2 C. Rice Krispies cereal
Dash red pepper or hot sauce (not
    too much or they'll be too hot!)

Mix all ingredients. Form into small balls. Flatten with fork dipped in water on a cookie sheet. Place slightly apart on cookie sheet and bake at 325° until lightly browned, approximately 12 to 14 minutes.

JILL'S CHEESE STRAWS

1/2 lb. salted Land 'O Lakes butter
1 lb. N.Y. State sharp cheese
3 1/2 C. self-rising flour, sifted
3 T. ice water
1/2 tsp. red pepper

Grate cheese and butter. (Let stand at room temperature.) Knead cheese, butter, red pepper and flour together. Use ice water as needed. Put in electric cookie cutter and spread on cookie sheet. Cut into 2 to 3" strips. Cook at 425° for 10 to 12 minutes. Watch carefully. They will burn quickly. Ones on the edge of pan might need to be removed first. Let cool on paper towels. Stack in airtight container.

Jill Patten McCurry
Wife of Pierce McCurry
(One of the Twelve)

SARA'S CHEESE STRAWS

3/4 lb. New York State sharp cheese
1 stick margarine, softened
1/2 tsp. salt
1 1/2 C. all-purpose flour
Cayenne pepper, to taste
   (start with 1/2 tsp.)

Grate cheese; add flour, salt and pepper. Mix well. Add softened margarine and mix well. Put in cookie press. Spread onto cookie sheet, cut in desired lengths and bake at 350° for 12 to 15 minutes.

Sara Winn
Manchester, GA

BAKED CHICKEN LIVERS

8 slices bacon, partially
   cooked and sliced in thirds
12 chicken livers, halved
   (to make 24 pieces)
1/2 tsp. sage
1/2 tsp. salt
1/4 tsp. pepper

Preheat oven to 450°. Wrap each chicken liver with 1/3 slice of bacon. Secure with a wooden toothpick. Place on a broiler pan (one with a rack over the pan) and bake until bacon is crisp.
Very unusual!

CHICKEN PUFFS

1 C. mayonnaise
2 C. cooked chicken, finely chopped
1 green onion, minced
1/2 tsp. seasoned salt
1/4 tsp. pepper
1/4 tsp. thyme
1/4 tsp. basil
3/4 C. Swiss cheese, grated
1/2 C. Parmesan cheese
Bread, cut in 24 rounds

Preheat oven to 350°. Mix first 9 ingredients until very well blended; spread equal amounts on 24 bread rounds. Bake on a foil-lined cookie sheet for 10 minutes. Makes 24 servings.

DEVILED PINWHEELS

1 lg. can deviled ham
2 tsp. chopped chives
10 slices white or wheat bread
2 T. melted butter

Trim crusts from bread. Roll each slice with a rolling pin until slightly flattened. Spread ham onto bread; sprinkle chives on top and roll up "jelly-roll" style; brush lightly with melted butter. Place on a plate, seam-side down; cover with plastic wrap. Chill for 2 or 3 hours, then slice in 1" thick pinwheels. Makes approximately 45.

HAM & CHEESE PINWHEELS

1 10-oz. pkg. Danish ham, sliced
1 8-oz. pkg. cream cheese,
    at room temperature
1 T. chopped chives

Separate slices of ham. Cream together cheese and chopped chives; spread mixture on each ham slice (one at a time) and roll jelly-roll style. Place each rolled up slice seam-side down on a plate and refrigerate until cheese has firmed again. Slice into 1/2" pinwheels. Serve on a glass plate, garnished with parsley sprigs or cilantro.

HAM DELIGHTS

1 lb. baked ham, shaved or shredded
1/3 lb. Swiss cheese, shredded
1 stick margarine, melted
3 T. prepared mustard
3 T. poppy seeds
1 tsp. Worcestershire sauce
1 med. onion, chopped or
    2 T. dried onion flakes
3 pkg. small party rolls
    (Pepperidge Farm brand)

Split each package of dinner rolls in half (in one piece). Spread mixture on bottom layer and replace tops of rolls (all in one piece). Return to metal pan or container. Bake at 325° for 10 to 15 minutes or until hot. (Heat just before serving.) Cut into individual sandwiches.

Can be made ahead and frozen. Just heat and serve.

Good for a brunch or luncheon or anytime.

HAM PUFFS

2 C. cooked ham, ground
2 T. mayonnaise
2 tsp. prepared mustard
1 1/2 tsp. prepared horseradish
1 tsp. minced green onion
30 toasted rounds (made by
    cutting rounds from bread)
    or 30 Melba toast rounds

Place ham in food processor or grinder, and mix until ham is smooth paste. Add remaining ingredients and blend well. Put equal amounts on toasted rounds or Melba toast. Broil until puffed and lightly browned. Makes 30 servings.

WRAPPED MELON BALLS

1/2 watermelon
1 cantaloupe
1 honeydew melon
1 T. lemon juice
1/4 lb. prosciutto ham, thinly sliced
Sprigs of fresh mint

Using a melon baller, scoop balls from each piece of fruit (as many as you need of each). Sprinkle with lemon juice. Wrap each ball with a thin strip of prosciutto ham. Secure with a toothpick. Chill and serve in hollowed out watermelon. Cut a slice off bottom of watermelon to sit flat.

OLIVES IN BLANKETS

1 3-oz. pkg. cream cheese
1/2 tsp. Worcestershire sauce
20 stuffed olives, drained and
    placed on a double layer
    of towels for 5 minutes
1/2 C. finely chopped nuts

Combine the cream cheese and Worcestershire sauce together until smooth. Cover each olive about 1/4" thick with cream cheese mixture; roll each olive in nuts. Chill for 1 hour before serving. Makes 20.

BOILED GREEN PEANUTS

3 lb. green peanuts in shells
3/4 C. salt
6 qt. boiling water

Wash peanuts (do not shell). In a large pot, bring water and salt to a rolling boil. Add the peanuts, reduce heat and boil slowly for 2½ to 3 hours or until peanuts are tender. Drain and serve hot or cold.

Note: For unusual flavor, add a ham hock to the boiling water. This makes the peanuts even better!

UNCLE PIERCE'S TOASTED PECANS

1 stick butter
1 1/2 to 2 lb. pecan halves
Salt

Put in 8x10" metal pan 1 stick butter, pecans and salt to taste. Cook at 250° for 1½ to 2 hours. Taste after 1 hour and add salt if necessary. Cook until done. (Do not overcook!!) Stir often during cooking.

For added flavor, sprinkle with garlic powder while cooking.

Pierce McCurry
(One of the Twelve)
Alpharetta, GA

CHOCOLATE POTATO CHIPS

8 oz. semi-sweet chocolate morsels*
2 tsp. liquid lecithin**
1 6-oz. pkg. rippled potato chips

Melt chocolate in top of double boiler over very hot (not boiling) water. Add lecithin and stir until smooth. Leave over hot water. Dip each chip individually in melted chocolate and place in single layer on 2 wax paper-lined cookie sheets. Let dry until chocolate is cooled completely. Store in airtight containers. Will make approximately 6 dozen.

Note: *Butterscotch morsels may be substituted for chocolate.

**Liquid lecithin is found at most health food stores.

CHILI RICE SNACKS

2/3 C. butter
1 tsp. salt
2 tsp. chili powder
8 C. Rice Chex cereal

Preheat oven to 300°. Place a large baking pan with high sides over medium heat. Melt the butter. Mix salt with chili powder; stir into butter and mix well. Add cereal, stirring gently until completely covered with butter mixture. Stir for 5 minutes over medium heat. Put baking pan in preheated oven for 10 to 15 minutes. Stir gently once or twice. Remove from oven and cool completely. Store in quart jars with lids. Makes 2 quarts.

Make one day ahead.

HOT COLD TOMATOES

6 to 8 lg. red, ripe tomatoes
   (in season is always best),
   peeled and sliced
4 jalapeno peppers, sliced
   in small rounds
Saltines
Hellmann's mayonnaise
Salt

Layer tomato slices and peppers in covered container. Refrigerate for 1 hour. Spread mayonnaise liberally on saltines. Top with a tomato slice and pepper round. Salt to taste. You won't need to add pepper!

Hot! Hot! Hot!
Good! Good! Good!
Warning: This recipe may become habit forming!

BAKED BEEF DIP

2 (2 1/2-oz.) jars dried beef, chopped
2 8-oz. pkg. cream cheese, softened
4 T. milk (or little more)
1 C. sour cream
1 med. onion, chopped
1/2 chopped green pepper (optional)
Dash pepper
1 C. chopped pecans

Combine and mix first 7 ingredients. Top with chopped pecans. Bake at 350° for 20 to 30 minutes.

Serve with crackers.

Lynda Rogers
Manchester, GA

- DIPS -

CHOCOLATE CABBAGE BOWL

1 lg. cabbage
8 oz. semi-sweet chocolate
1 scant T. vegetable shortening

Remove outer leaves of cabbage (5 or 6 of them will do). Rinse in cold water; pat dry. Melt chocolate and shortening in top of double boiler. Using a large spoon, coat one side of each cabbage leaf and place in a single layer on a wax paper-lined cookie sheet. Chill until chocolate is firm. Peel cabbage leaf off for a perfect chocolate leaf. Scoop out cabbage center leaving at least 1 1/2" on bottom and sides. Cut bottom to sit flat. Secure chocolate cabbage leaves to outer side of scooped out cabbage with toothpick to look natural.

Fill cavity of cabbage with sweet dip or dip of choice according to what you'll be dipping in it.

Everyone will love it!

BASIC HERB DIP

1 C. buttermilk
1 C. mayonnaise
1/2 tsp. pepper
1 1/2 tsp. seasoned salt
1/2 tsp. dried minced garlic
1 T. instant onion
1 T. parsley flakes

Mix ingredients in order listed. Cover and refrigerate for at least 1 hour. Makes 2 cups.

Good dip for anything at all.

CRAB DIP MOLD

1 env. plain gelatin
1/2 C. water
1 can cream of mushroom soup
1 lg. pkg. cream cheese
1 C. mayonnaise
1 C. chopped celery
1 C. chopped green onions
1 to 1 1/2 lb. crab or shrimp

Mix gelatin and water. Heat soup to boiling and add gelatin. Cool a little. Add cream cheese. Add rest of ingredients. Pour in Jell-O or "Bundt pan" mold. Refrigerate to set.

Serve with Carr's water crackers or any bland cracker.

HOT CRAB DIP

1 lb. crab meat, drained
1 lg. pkg. cream cheese
1 med. onion, chopped fine
1 T. horseradish
3 T. milk
Dash of salt and pepper
Slivered almonds

Blend cream cheese, onion, horseradish and milk in blender. Fold in crab meat, salt and pepper. Put in baking dish; sprinkle with slivered almonds and bake at 350° for 20 minutes. Serve hot with crackers.

DILLY DIP

1 C. sour cream
1/2 C. mayonnaise
1 T. dillweed
1 tsp. onion powder
1 tsp. seasoned salt

Mix all ingredients. Refrigerate for 3 to 6 hours. Makes 1 1/2 cups.
Wonderful with raw vegetables!

FRUIT DIP

1 8-oz. pkg. cream cheese, softened
1 7-oz. jar marshmallow creme
1 T. orange juice
2 T. orange marmalade

Mix all ingredients. Chill thoroughly. Makes approximately 1 1/2 cups.
Serve with assorted fresh fruits.

PINEAPPLE CHEESE DIP

8 oz. Velveeta cheese, cut in 1" cubes
1/2 C. crushed pineapple, drained
1/4 C. juice (from can
    of crushed pineapple)
1 tsp. curry powder

In a 1-quart glass bowl, combine all ingredients and microwave 2 to 4 minutes on High. Stir once after each minute of cooking until cheese is melted.
Good with hot "finger" size sticks of cooked ham or as a dip for cooked chicken wings or cooked chicken strips.

SPICY RO-TEL SAUCE

1 1/2 lb. lean ground beef,
   browned and drained
1 can Ro-Tel tomatoes,
   chopped by hand
1/2 lb. Velveeta cheese
Tortilla chips

Brown ground beef in a skillet; drain. Cut Velveeta in 1" cubes and combine with Ro-Tel tomatoes. Place in microwave and cook until cheese melts. Stir several times during cooking time. Mix with ground beef.

Serve hot. Dip with large tortilla chips. Smooth and spicy. Everyone will want your recipe.

Note: This can be a main dish served over hot, cooked white rice.

Stacey Cooper Radford
Lincolnton, GA

SPINACH DIP

1 10-oz. pkg. frozen, chopped spinach,
   thawed and drained thoroughly
1 8-oz. ctn. sour cream
1 C. mayonnaise
1 can water chestnuts,
   drained and chopped
1 pkg. dry vegetable soup mix
1 bunch green onions, minced

Mix all ingredients in a glass bowl; cover and chill for 3 to 6 hours. Makes 2 1/2 cups.

Serve with crackers or vegetable sticks.

VEGETABLE DIP (LO-CAL)

1 10-oz. pkg. frozen, chopped
   spinach, drained
1 16-oz. ctn. cottage cheese
1/4 C. no-fat mayonnaise
1 env. instant vegetable soup mix (dry)
1/2 tsp. dried dill
Dash of nutmeg
Dash of seasoned salt

Place thawed spinach in a plate; place another plate on top of spinach and press plates together to squeeze spinach dry. Pour liquid away. In a blender or food processor, puree cottage cheese. In a large mixing bowl, combine drained spinach, pureed cottage cheese and remaining ingredients. Makes about 3 cups.

- SPREADS -

BLUE/BLUEBERRY SPREAD

4 oz. cream cheese
3 tsp. blue cheese
1/2 C. blueberries, drained well
1 T. powdered sugar

Combine all ingredients. Chill. Garnish with blueberries.

Serve as spread with lemon thins or brown-edged cookies. Very tart!

BLUE VELVET

4 oz. blue cheese
1 stick butter
2 T. cream sherry
1/2 C. finely chopped walnuts

Cream cheese and butter. Add sherry and blend well. Shape in a ball by rolling in palms of hands. Roll in chopped nuts. Makes 1 cup.
Spread on crackers.

CARROT CRUNCH SPREAD

3 lg. carrots, grated fine
3/4 C. salted peanuts, chopped
1 rib celery, chopped fine
3/4 C. mayonnaise
1/4 tsp. tarragon

Combine all ingredients. Chill.
Spread on trimmed bread or crackers.

CHEESE CARROTS

1/2 lb. Cheddar cheese, grated
2 oz. cream cheese, softened
1/2 tsp. paprika
Parsley sprigs

Combine grated cheese with paprika. By tablespoonfuls, roll cheese into shape of small carrot. Place parsley sprig in stem end. Chill until serving. Makes approximately 15.
Note: May also be made into a bunch of carrots (5 or 6), made actual size of carrots or slightly smaller, with one big bunch of parsley to resemble carrot top. Use as cheese spread.

GEORGIA CHEESE PEACHES

1/2 lb. sharp Cheddar cheese,
   grated finely
4 oz. cream cheese, softened
2 T. peach jam
Paprika
Mint sprigs with leaves or peach
   leaves (if you can get them)
3/4 C. peach jam
1/2 tsp. dried mint or
   1 tsp. fresh chopped mint

Combine Cheddar cheese, cream cheese and 2 tablespoons of jam until smooth. Divide into two equal parts. One at a time, roll between palms and shape like a peach. Place a little paprika in a plate and barely roll "front" side of "peach" in it so the coloring is similar to the real thing. Stick mint or peach leaves in top. Chill.
Use as a spread on crackers. Very good when cheese is spread first, then topped with peach jam mixed with mint.

OPEN FACE CREAM CHEESE SANDWICHES

8 oz. cream cheese, softened
1/2 C. mayonnaise
1/2 C. finely chopped,
　　stuffed green olives
1/2 C. finely chopped toasted nuts
A few grains of cayenne pepper
A few dashes of Worcestershire sauce
A few dashes of hickory salt (optional)

Mix well. Spread on small rounds or desired shapes of bread. Top with slice of stuffed olive.

Flo Pursley
Lincolnton, GA

PARTY RYES

1 C. grated Cheddar cheese
1/2 C. mayonnaise
1/4 C. chopped green onions
　　(and some tops)
1/4 tsp. curry powder
1/2 C. chopped black olives

Mix and spread on party rye; broil and watch until bubbly.

EGG SALAD FILLING

6 hard-boiled eggs, mashed with
　　tines of fork until crumbly
1/2 C. mayonnaise
1 tsp. chives (dried)
1/2 tsp. salt
1/4 tsp. pepper
1/4 tsp. paprika
1/2 C. chopped stuffed olives or
　　1/2 C. sweet pickle relish
1 T. mustard

Combine eggs and other ingredients in a mixing bowl. Mix well. Spread on bread for sandwiches or on crackers. Serves 4.

TEA SANDWICH SPREAD

1/2 C. orange juice
1 T. lemon juice
1 apple, cored and cut in small pieces
1 C. raisins
1 C. walnuts
Dash of seasoned salt

Place all ingredients in either a blender or food processor. Mix until a spreadable consistency. Spread on trimmed bread cut in pretty shapes.

VEGETABLE CHEESE SPREAD

1/2 C. French dressing
1/4 lb. sharp Cheddar cheese, cubed
1/2 cucumber, unpeeled, cut in fourths
1 carrot, sliced
1/2 tsp. seasoned salt
1/4 tsp. celery seed
1/3 C. sun-dried tomatoes
Chopped parsley, for garnish
    (optional)

Combine all ingredients in blender or food processor until vegetables are in very small pieces. Spread on small bread rounds or crisp crackers. Garnish with parsley. Makes 1 1/2 cups.

CRAB SPREAD

1 1/2 C. Hellmann's mayonnaise
1 1/2 C. fresh crab meat, flaked or
    canned crab meat, drained
1/2 C. French dressing
3/4 C. shredded sharp
    Cheddar cheese
1 1/2 tsp. prepared horseradish
A few grains of cayenne
1/4 tsp. salt
Dash of mace

Mix all ingredients together. Stir well. Place in a tightly covered bowl and chill for several hours. Makes approximately 2 1/2 cups.

Serve with assorted crackers. Very good on Waverly wafers.

CRUNCHY CRAB SPREAD

1/2 lb. fresh crab or 1 can King crab
2 sm. pkg. chive cream cheese
3 T. sour cream
2 T. mayonnaise
Juice of 1 whole lemon
1 can water chestnuts (tuna can size),
    chopped fine
2 green onions, chopped
1 clove garlic, smashed
1 tsp. Worcestershire sauce
Salt, to taste

Combine all ingredients and refrigerate. Serve with crackers.

Can be used as a dip if you add more sour cream and mayonnaise.

LOBSTER OR VARIETY MOLD

1 (10 1/2-oz.) can condensed
   tomato soup (undiluted)
1 8-oz. pkg. cream cheese
2 env. unflavored gelatin
1/4 C. cold water
1 C. mayonnaise
3/4 C. finely chopped celery
1 lg. onion, minced
1 tsp. salt
1 lb. lobster meat*
2 dashes hot sauce
1/2 tsp. paprika
1 tsp. Worcestershire sauce
2 tsp. prepared white horseradish

*Crab meat, shrimp, tuna, salmon, minced clams, minced ham or 1/2 pound sharp cheese (grated) substitute quite well for the lobster.

Heat soup and into it thoroughly blend cream cheese. Soften unflavored gelatin in cold water. Dissolve gelatin in hot soup mixture; cool. Then add remaining ingredients. Mix well. Place in a lightly greased 1½-quart mold and chill until firm. Unmold and serve with crackers.

Beechie McCurry Miller
(One of the Twelve)
Charleston, SC

SMOKED OYSTER LOG

1 flat can smoked oysters
1 8-oz. pkg. cream cheese, softened
1/2 tsp. Tabasco sauce
1 tsp. lemon juice (optional)
1/2 C. chopped fresh parsley
   or 2 T. chopped parsley
1 T. chopped chives (fresh or dried)
Paprika, to garnish

Drain oysters. Mash with tines of fork until fairly smooth. In a plate, combine softened cream cheese with oysters; mix well. Add Tabasco and lemon juice. Shape into a small "log". Put chopped parsley and chives in another plate and roll log in mixture until well coated. Sprinkle on a little paprika. Wrap in plastic wrap and refrigerate 3 hours or overnight. Serve with crackers.

SHRIMP PASTE

1/4 C. sherry
1 1/2 T. lemon juice
1 stick softened butter
2 tsp. Dijon mustard
1/2 tsp. salt
1/4 tsp. mace
3 drops Tabasco sauce
1 lb. shrimp, cooked,
   shelled and deveined

Using a food processor or blender, combine all ingredients. Be sure to add just a few shrimp at a time to the butter mixture. Serve on toast points or crisp crackers.

VELVETINE SHRIMP

1/2 lb. shrimp, cooked,
    cooled and peeled
1/4 lb. softened butter
2 tsp. chopped chives
Few grains of cayenne pepper

Mash shrimp fine with tines of fork. Cream in butter; add chives and cayenne pepper. Pack in a crock or mold that has been lightly coated with mayonnaise. Chill. Serve on Melba toast rounds or crackers of choice.

FRENCH TOASTED SANDWICHES

Dip the sandwiches in the following being sure to coat well: 1 beaten egg with 2 tablespoons milk. (This mixture is enough to make 2 French Toasted Sandwiches.) Brown slowly on both sides in 1 tablespoon of melted margarine in a heavy skillet. Slice in half to form 2 triangle shaped sandwiches or in 3 "finger" shaped pieces. Makes 2 sandwiches -- any kind!

QUARTERBACK SNEAK SANDWICH

4 French bread rolls, split
Butter or margarine
4 frozen cube steaks
4 onion slices, separated into rings
1 (15 1/2-oz.) can chili with beans,
    heated

Spread rolls with butter or margarine; toast. Pan fry steaks according to package directions. For each sandwich, place a steak on half of roll; top with onion rings, chili, and top of roll. Makes 4 sandwiches.

- BEVERAGES -

CAFE SAVANNAH

24 marshmallows, cut in quarters
1 T. instant coffee granules
1 C. boiling water
1 C. whipping cream, whipped stiff
1/2 C. chopped pecans
Sprigs of mint, for garnish

Dissolve coffee in boiling water. Pour over marshmallows and stir until dissolved into smooth mixture. Cool. Fold whipped cream and nuts into mixture. Pour into 6 sherbet glasses. Garnish with sprigs of mint. Chill for 3 hours. Makes 6 servings.

A light dessert -- perfect after a heavy meal.

CHARLESTON TOMATO JUICE

1 8-oz. can tomato juice, chilled
Dash of salt and pepper
Sherry

Pour juice in glasses. Add salt and pepper. Add 1 teaspoon sherry and a few drops of Worcestershire sauce. Garnish with a twist of lemon.

INSTANT HOT CHOCOLATE MIX

1/2 C. confectioner's sugar
1 8-qt. bx. powdered milk
1 sm. jar Pream or Coffee-mate
1 16-oz. bx. Nestle Quik (chocolate)

Combine ingredients. Mix well. Store in airtight container. Use 2 tablespoons per cup of hot chocolate. Add more or less if you like.

Betty Miller Wilkins
Prosperity, SC

KAHLUA

4 C. sugar
4 C. water
1 2-oz. jar instant coffee
1/5 vodka
2 vanilla beans (or estimate
    vanilla flavor)

Boil sugar and water for 5 minutes. Remove from heat. Add instant coffee and stir until dissolved. Cool; add vodka. Slit vanilla bean lengthwise and drop into gallon jug. Pour mixture into jug and let stand 14 days. Shake each day. (If vanilla flavoring is used, unnecessary to stand 14 days.) If vanilla beans are used, after 14 days strain mixture into smaller bottles. Keep one in refrigerator.

After dinner drink or poured over vanilla ice cream.

CEDAR HILL RUM PUNCH

2 1/2 C. unsweetened
    orange juice, chilled
2 1/2 C. unsweetened
    pineapple juice, chilled
2 1/2 C. apricot nectar
2 1/2 C. unsweetened lime juice
2 1/2 C. rum or 2 oz. rum flavoring
1 bot. maraschino cherries with stems

Mix chilled juices with rum. Serve over ice in frosted glasses or punch cups. Place a cherry in each glass or cup. Makes 20 servings.

ICED TEA PUNCH

1 qt. tea
1 pt. ginger ale
1/2 pt. water
1 1/2 C. Welch's grape juice
Juice of 1 lemon
Juice of 1 orange
Sprigs of mint, lemon slices and
    orange slices, for garnish

Brew tea with a few sprigs of mint added. Strain. Chill. When ready to serve, add water and juices. Garnish each glass with lemon and orange slices and sprigs of mint. Serve in tall glasses of ice.

PINA COLADA PUNCH

1 46-oz. bot. white grape juice, chilled
1 32-oz. bot. ginger ale with lemon, chilled
1 36-oz. bot. pina colada mix, chilled
1 C. rum or 1 1/2 T. rum flavoring

Mix ingredients in a large container just before serving. Serve from a pitcher or a punch bowl into glasses or punch cups filled with ice. Serves 25 to 30.

PRISSY'S PUNCH

1 46-oz. can pineapple juice
1 6-oz. can frozen concentrated orange juice
3 sm. pkg. lime Kool-Aid
2 C. granulated sugar
2 drops green food color
Water
1 bot. ginger ale, chilled
1 sm. bot. almond flavoring

Mix first 5 ingredients in a gallon container. Add enough water to make 1 gallon. Chill.

When ready to serve, pour into a punch bowl; add ginger ale and almond flavoring. Use ice or ice ring in punch bowl.

TERESA'S FROZEN PUNCH

2 46-oz. cans pineapple juice
1 1/2 C. granulated sugar
1 tsp. almond flavoring
1 qt. ginger ale

Dissolve sugar in 1/2 cup pineapple juice; add remaining juice and almond flavoring. Freeze. Take out of freezer 1 to 2 hours before serving. Add ginger ale when ready to serve.

Teresa McCurry Tankersley
Lincolnton, GA

Soups, Salads & Dressings Preserving

AUNT SYLVIA'S BROCCOLI SOUP

3 T. oil
3/4 C. chopped onion
3 C. chicken broth
2 C. water
8 oz. fine egg noodles
2 10-oz. pkg. frozen broccoli
1 tsp. salt
1/8 tsp. garlic powder
Pepper, to taste
6 C. whole milk
1 1/2 lb. Velveeta cheese

Heat oil; saute onion; add chicken broth, water, noodles and salt. Cook until tender; add broccoli and garlic powder. Cook broccoli until just tender. Add milk, cheese and pepper. Simmer and serve in heated bowls. Serves 8 to 10.

Sylvia Herring McCurry
(One of the Twelve)
Lincolnton, GA

SARA'S SWEET AND SOUR CABBAGE SOUP

1 med. cabbage, cut up
2 cans stewed tomatoes
2 cans water
1 lb. stew beef, cut in 1 1/2" pieces
1 pkg. dried onion soup
3 T. granulated sugar
3 T. brown sugar
2 T. lemon juice
Salt and pepper, to taste

Brown beef in large soup pot; add salt and pepper to taste. Add tomatoes and remaining ingredients. Cover and cook slowly on low to medium heat. Makes 8 to 10 servings.

Sara Winn
Manchester, GA

CATFISH STEW

1/2 C. fatback, diced
1 med. onion, diced
2 lg. potatoes, diced
Water, to cover potatoes
1 lg. can whole tomatoes (Hunt's)
1 lb. skinless, boneless fish
1 C. (more or less) catsup
Salt
Pepper (red and black)
Sugar

In large boiler, fry fatback until crisp. Stir in onion and cook until golden brown. Add potatoes and just cover with water and let simmer until potatoes are soft. Chop tomatoes and add to mixture. Let come to boil, then turn to medium heat and add chopped fish. Add catsup and season to taste with pepper, salt and sugar. Cover and let simmer. Stir. Serve hot.

Patsy McCurry Partridge
(One of the Twelve)
Lincolnton, GA

CHEDDAR CHEESE SOUP

1/2 C. chopped onions
1/2 stick butter or margarine
4 T. flour
1 1/2 T. cornstarch
2 cans chicken broth
1 qt. milk
1 C. finely chopped carrots, cooked
1 C. finely chopped celery, cooked
1/4 tsp. paprika
1/2 tsp. seasoned salt
3/4 lb. sharp Cheddar cheese
Chopped parsley, to garnish

In a large, heavy pot, saute onions in butter until soft and transparent (not browned). Stir in flour and cornstarch. Mix well. Gradually add chicken broth and milk. Stir all the while. When this reaches the boiling point, add remaining ingredients. Reduce heat to low and simmer until soup is smooth and cheese is melted. Serve hot. Garnish with chopped parsley.

ATLANTA CLAMATO SOUP

2 C. beef broth
2 C. clam-tomato drink juice
1 C. dry white wine
1/2 C. dry sherry
1 green onion, finely chopped
1/8 tsp. instant garlic flakes
1/2 tsp. dried thyme

Combine all ingredients in saucepan; bring to a boil. Boil for 2 minutes. Serve hot with a twist of lemon and/or a sprig of fresh mint for garnish. Yield: 4 servings.
Soothes the soul.

CLAM CHOWDER

3 slices bacon, chopped
1 C. chopped onion
2 C. diced potatoes
1 C. water
1 tsp. salt
1/8 tsp. pepper
1 pt. clams, shucked and minced
    or 2 10-oz. cans minced clams
    (reserve juice)
2 C. Half and Half
2 T. butter
Dash ground mace

In a large, heavy saucepan, saute bacon until crisp. Add onions and cook 4 or 5 minutes. Add potatoes, salt, pepper and water. Cook uncovered until tender. Drain clams (reserve juice). Add chopped clams, 1/2 cup juice, Half and Half and butter. Stir well. Heat for 4 or 5 minutes. Be sure not to boil. Makes 4 to 6 servings.

CORN CHEESE CHOWDER

2 T. butter
1 onion, thinly sliced
1/2 C. chopped celery
3 C. peeled, cooked potatoes, diced
Salt and pepper, to taste
1/2 tsp. paprika
2 C. milk
1 16-oz. can cream-style corn
2 C. shredded Cheddar cheese
Parsley, to garnish

Melt butter; saute onion and celery just until tender. Add potatoes, milk, corn and seasonings. Heat to serving temperature. Remove from heat and stir in cheese until melted. Garnish with parsley. Yield: 6 servings.

Good on a cold day with cornbread.

CHURCH STREET CRAB SOUP

1 10-oz. can cream of mushroom soup
1 10-oz. can cream of asparagus soup
1 C. Half and Half cream
1 (7 1/2-oz.) can crab meat, flaked
1 tsp. Worcestershire sauce
1/4 tsp. ground mace
3 T. sherry
1/2 C. whipping cream

Combine soups, milk, crab meat, Worcestershire sauce, mace and sherry in saucepan; heat through. Add cream and warm to serving temperature. Yield: 4 servings.

MILK TOAST

4 T. butter or margarine
4 T. flour
1 tsp. salt
1/4 tsp. pepper
1/8 tsp. garlic salt
1 qt. milk, heated

In a skillet, combine butter, flour and 1 cup of the hot milk. Stir constantly. Add the remaining milk, salt, pepper and garlic salt. Toast 8 slices of bread. Place 2 slices, cut in half, on serving plate and pour hot mixture over toast. Serve immediately. Makes 4 servings.

Variation: Chipped, dried beef may be added to the hot mixture. Good Sunday night dish. Creamy and comforting! Feels like a hug.

OKRA SOUP

1 lg. beef shank
4 qt. water
Salt and pepper
3 qt. fresh okra, cut small
2 #2 cans tomatoes
1 lg. onion, chopped
1 tsp. sugar
1 tsp. dried basil

Boil beef in water until tender. Add remaining ingredients. Cover. Cook on low for 5 hours. Add more water if needed. Makes approximately 5 quarts.

POTATO SOUP

1 lg. onion, peeled and chopped or
    4 green onions, chopped
    (with tops)
1/2 stick butter or margarine
1 1/2 qt. hot water
5 med. potatoes, peeled and cubed
Salt and pepper, to taste
1 tsp. tarragon
1 lg. can evaporated milk, heated
    or 1 lg. can evaporated
    skim milk, heated
1/2 C. chopped parsley, for garnish

In a Dutch oven or large pot, saute onions in butter until transparent (do not brown). Add hot water, potatoes, salt, pepper and tarragon. Cook until potatoes are tender, but not soft. Add heated cream and simmer. Do not boil after adding cream. Serve in heated bowls, garnished with parsley.

Note: Good when your cupboard is almost bare. If you keep onions, potatoes and a can of evaporated milk on hand all the time, you won't ever "go hungry".

SEAFOOD STEW

1 lb. hot smoked sausage,
    cut in 1" slices
4 ears corn, husks removed,
    broken in half
2 lb. fresh shrimp, washed
    in cold water
1 tsp. salt
2 T. Old Bay Crab-Shrimp Boil
    seasoning
1 12-oz. bot. beer or 1 1/2 C. water

In a large, deep pot, layer as follows: Sausage slices, corn, shrimp, salt, and Old Bay seasoning. Pour beer or water over all and bring to a boil. Reduce heat; cover and cook until shrimp are pink. Stir so that all shrimp and sausage slices are cooked evenly. Don't overcook. Drain. Serve immediately in a large, shallow dish. Makes 4 servings.

See Sauce section for recipe if you want to dip the shrimp in something or just use prepared cocktail sauce.

ZUCCHINI SOUP

1 stick butter or margarine
1 med. onion, minced
8 sm. zucchini squash, sliced
3 C. chicken broth
1/2 C. Half and Half cream
1/4 lb. Velveeta cheese
Few grains cayenne pepper
Salt and pepper, to taste
Sprigs of parsley, to garnish
Croutons

Melt butter; saute onion and zucchini until tender. Add chicken broth. Simmer for 20 minutes. Remove from heat. Cool slightly and puree in blender or food processor. Return to pan. Add remaining ingredients and heat. Do not let boil. Serve in heated soup bowls garnished with parsley and topped with croutons.

- FRUIT SALADS -

APPLE-RAISIN SALAD

2 red apples
2 green apples
1/2 C. golden raisins
1/4 C. Hellmann's mayonnaise
1/2 C. finely chopped celery

Peel and dice apples; let stand in salted water a few minutes. Drain apples; pat dry. In bowl, combine apples, celery and raisins with mayonnaise. Serve on lettuce leaf. Serves 6.

BUTTERMILK SALAD

1 3-oz. pkg. orange Jell-O
1 sm. can crushed pineapple, drained
1/2 C. water
1 C. buttermilk
1 8-oz. ctn. Cool Whip
1/2 C. chopped pecans

In a saucepan, combine dry Jell-O, drained pineapple and water; heat until Jell-O dissolves; cool. Fold in rest of ingredients. Pour into one large mold or individual molds that have been rubbed with a little mayonnaise. Chill until set. Serve on a leaf of lettuce.

CUPCAKE SALAD

1 8-oz. ctn. dairy sour cream
2 T. lemon juice
3/4 C. granulated sugar
1/8 tsp. salt
1 9-oz. can crushed pineapple,
    drained well
1/4 C. bottled red cherries, chopped
1/2 C. pecans, finely chopped
1 banana, sliced thin

In a mixing bowl, combine sour cream, lemon juice, sugar and salt. Add remaining ingredients. Stir well. Line 8 muffin tins with cupcake papers. Pour mixture into papers and freeze until firm. When ready to serve, remove the paper liners and serve on a leaf of lettuce. Garnish each with half a cherry or 1 whole maraschino cherry. If you wish to store these, remove from tins after freezing, place in Ziploc bag and return to freezer.
Note: Any frozen salad may be made in this manner.

PEAR OR PEACH SALAD

1 #2 can pear halves or
    peach halves, drained
Mayonnaise
3/4 C. shredded Cheddar cheese
Lettuce leaves

Drain pears or peaches. Place each on a lettuce leaf. Place 1/2 to 1 teaspoon of mayonnaise in cavity and top with shredded cheese. Cover and refrigerate until ready to serve. Serves 4 to 6.
Note: Pineapple rings may also be used.

SARA'S PEAR SALAD

1 sm. pkg. orange Jell-O
1 lg. can pears, drained and chopped
   (reserve juice)
2 C. pear juice
1 8-oz. ctn. cream cheese
1 9-oz. ctn. Cool Whip

Heat pear juice. Dissolve Jell-O in hot juice. Cool. Refrigerate until slightly congealed. In a large bowl, combine cream cheese and Cool Whip. Mix well. Add to Jell-O mixture. Stir gently. Fold in pears. Refrigerate overnight.

Sara Winn
Manchester, GA

PISTACHIO PUDDING SALAD

2 sm. pkg. pistachio
   instant pudding (dry)
1 #2 can crushed pineapple
1 C. miniature marshmallows
1 C. coconut
1 lg. ctn. Cool Whip
1/2 C. chopped nuts

Combine all ingredients in a large bowl. Pour into a 9x13" rectangular dish; chill and serve.

Brenda Edmunds Chatham
Jacksonville, FL

TWENTY FOUR HOUR FRUIT SALAD

3 T. sugar
3 T. vinegar
2 eggs
1 T. butter
1 can evaporated milk or
   1/3 pt. whipping cream
1 bot. red cherries
Juice of 1 lemon
1 can fruit cocktail
1 can sliced pineapple
1 C. chopped nuts
1 bag small marshmallows

Cook sugar, vinegar, eggs and butter in double boiler until thick. Cool. Whip milk until stiff; add juice of 1 lemon. Mix in fruits. Fold in nuts. Refrigerate.

Joann McCurry Ferguson
(One of the Twelve)
Lincolnton, GA

- SLAWS -

CASHEW CABBAGE SLAW (SWEET)

2 heads cabbage
40 sm. marshmallows
1 #2 can pineapple bits
1 sm. bot. maraschino cherries,
　　cut in halves
1/2 lb. salted cashew nuts, for garnish

Dressing:
1/2 pt. whipping cream,
　　whipped until stiff
1 C. mayonnaise
1/2 tsp. salt
1 tsp. prepared mustard

Wash cabbage. Drain well. Slice fine. In a large bowl, combine cabbage, marshmallows, pineapple, cherries and Dressing. Chill thoroughly. Serve on a large platter. Toss cashew nuts over salad just before serving.

Combine ingredients.

FRUIT AND VEGETABLE SLAW

2 carrots, grated
1 rib celery, sliced paper thin
1/2 med. cabbage, shredded
1/2 C. chopped, dried fruit
1/2 C. chopped walnuts
1/2 C. Honey Dijon dressing*

*More if needed to moisten other ingredients.
　　Combine all ingredients and chill until ready to serve. Serves 4 to 6.

MARINATED COLESLAW

1 lg. cabbage, shredded
1 lg. onion, chopped fine
1 green pepper, chopped fine
1 C. sugar
1 C. salad oil
1 C. cider vinegar
1 tsp. dry mustard
1 tsp. celery seed
1 tsp. salt
Black pepper

Mix vegetables together in large bowl. Sprinkle sugar over them; do not stir. Bring remaining ingredients to a rolling boil, pour over the vegetables, cover and refrigerate. Stir after 12 hours and once a day thereafter. Ready to eat.
　　Keeps several weeks.

Beth Radford Ashmore
Lincolnton, GA

SUPER SLAW

1 lg. head raw cabbage, shredded
2 C. cooked ham, chopped
1 lg. onion, minced
Salt and pepper, to taste
1/2 tsp. dry mustard
1 C. mayonnaise
1 egg white, beaten until frothy
1 T. sugar
1 T. white vinegar

Shred cabbage into large mixing bowl. Add ham and onions. Refrigerate until just before serving. About 5 to 10 minutes before serving, beat the egg white. Fold it into the mayonnaise; add sugar, vinegar, mustard, salt and pepper. Add this to the slaw mixture and toss until moistened. Makes 8 to 10 servings.

- VEGETABLE SALADS -

OLD FASHIONED BEET SALAD

1 qt. chopped, cooked beets
1 qt. chopped cabbage
3/4 C. ground horseradish
2 C. sugar
1 T. salt
Vinegar

Mix beets and cabbage. Stir in sugar, salt and horseradish; cover with vinegar. Mix well; cover. Place in refrigerator.
Will keep for several weeks.

SUNFLOWER BROCCOLI SALAD

1 lb. fresh broccoli
1/2 C. golden raisins
1 sm. red onion, thinly sliced into rings
4 slices bacon, cooked,
    drained and crumbled
1 3-oz. pkg. cream cheese, softened
2 T. sugar
2 T. white vinegar
2 T. vegetable oil
1 T. prepared mustard
1 clove garlic, minced fine
2 T. shelled sunflower seeds,
    for garnish

Wash broccoli, trim stems and break flowerets into small pieces. Slice tender stems into 1/4" rounds. Drain well. Combine broccoli, raisins, onion rings and 1/2 of crumbled bacon. Mix slightly and set aside. Combine cream cheese, sugar, vinegar, oil, mustard and garlic. Blend well and pour over broccoli mixture. Refrigerate at least 3 hours. Just before serving, sprinkle with remaining bacon and sunflower seeds. Makes 6 to 8 servings.

CUCUMBER SALAD

1 T. grated onion
1 C. cottage cheese
1 C. mayonnaise
1 C. grated cucumber
1 sm. pkg. lime Jell-O
1/2 C. finely chopped nuts
3/4 C. boiling water

Dissolve Jell-O in boiling water; add cottage cheese, mayonnaise, then add remaining ingredients. Pour in mold (lightly coated with mayonnaise) or in small individual molds. Invert individual molded salad on leaf of lettuce. Garnish with twist of lime.

Beatrice McCurry Miller
(One of the Twelve)
Charleston, SC

RAW MUSHROOM SALAD

1 lb. raw, fresh mushrooms, wash,
    dry, slice from rounded top
    through stems
Celery (center stalks), cut
    in bite-size pieces
2 hard-cooked eggs, cut in 1/8
2 T. minced green onions, tops and all
2 minced whole pimiento peppers
Season, to taste with salt and
    fresh ground pepper

French Dressing:

Combine ingredients. Shake Dressing well and pour over mushroom mixture; toss lightly and serve on Romaine or leaf lettuce.

Combine 2 parts olive oil, 2 parts salad oil to 1 part wine vinegar.

Betty Miller Wilkins
Prosperity, SC

ORANGE ONION SALAD

6 seedless oranges
1 med. red onion
4 oz. French dressing or
    Russian dressing
1 T. poppy seeds

Peel and section oranges. Peel onion and slice into paper thin rings. Place onions and oranges in a shallow glass bowl. Mix dressing with poppy seeds and pour over top. Refrigerate for 1 hour. Stir just before serving. Makes 6 to 8 servings.

Unusual and delicious with pork and poultry.

MISS MILLIE'S OVERNIGHT SALAD

1 med. head lettuce, torn
   in bite-size pieces
2 10-oz. pkg. frozen English peas
   (uncooked)
1 C. mayonnaise
2 bunches green onions, thinly sliced
2 C. grated cheese (sharp Cheddar)

In a 9x13" rectangular dish (glass or Tupperware), place lettuce on bottom. Combine peas, mayonnaise and onions. Spread over lettuce. Top with grated cheese. Cover tightly and refrigerate overnight. Serve with a large spoon.

Freshly ground black pepper adds a nice touch when serving.

Millie Ashmore
Lincolnton, GA

BOOM BOOM'S DELUXE POTATO SALAD

6 lb. med. potatoes,
   cooked and cooled

In boiling, salted water to cover, cook unpared potatoes, covered, just until tender, about 30 minutes. Drain; refrigerate until cold.

Dressing:
3 C. mayonnaise or
   cooked salad dressing
1 1/2 C. finely chopped onion
1 1/2 C. cubed, pared cucumber
1 C. coarsely chopped green pepper
1 4-oz. can pimientos,
   drained and diced
2/3 C. sliced sweet gherkins
1/3 C. pickle juice
3 T. cider vinegar
2 T. salt

Combine ingredients in a mixing bowl. Stir well.

Peel and cube potatoes (or slice in 1/4" rounds). Pour Dressing over potatoes and mix gently until potatoes are moistened. Garnish of choice.

Betty Miller Wilkins
Prosperity, SC

Garnish:
Celery leaves
Cherry tomatoes
Ripe olives

COUSIN DONNA'S POTATO SALAD

7 lg. potatoes, peeled and cubed
2 hard-boiled eggs, mashed fine
1 bell pepper, chopped
1 sm. onion, minced
1 sm. jar pimiento,
   drained and chopped
1 C. mayonnaise
2 tsp. mustard
Salt and pepper, to taste
Paprika, for garnish

In a large pot, boil potatoes slowly for approximately 20 minutes. Rinse potatoes with cold water; drain and set aside. In a large bowl, crumble eggs with fork and mix in remaining ingredients. Add potatoes and stir gently until well blended. Garnish with paprika.

Donna McCurry Crook
Lincolnton, GA

Hospitality Southern Style

HOT SPINACH SALAD

6 slices bacon
1/4 C. vinegar
2 T. water
1/2 tsp. salt
1/4 tsp. pepper
1/4 tsp. dry mustard
3/4 lb. fresh spinach
4 green onions, sliced
1 C. fresh mushrooms, sliced
1 hard-cooked egg, grated

Fry bacon until crisp; remove from drippings and drain on paper toweling. To bacon drippings, add vinegar, water, salt, pepper and mustard. Cook until mixture boils. Toss spinach, onions and mushrooms in salad bowl. Pour hot dressing over and toss gently. Garnish with grated egg and crumbled bacon. Yield: 4 servings.

SPINACH SALAD WITH STRAWBERRIES

1 lg. bunch fresh spinach
1 pt. strawberries
1 C. cider vinegar
1 C. light brown sugar
1/4 tsp. celery seed

Wash spinach (drain well). Tear into large bite-size pieces. Wash and drain strawberries. Remove stems and slice from top to bottom. Mix with spinach, cover and refrigerate. In a small saucepan or in microwave, heat vinegar, sugar and celery seed until thin syrup consistency. Cool and pour over salad.
Makes a beautiful salad!

SPINACH STRAWBERRY SALAD

8 to 10 C. fresh spinach,
    washed and drained well
1 1/2 C. sliced, fresh
    strawberries, hulled

Tear drained spinach leaves in bite-size pieces. Place in bowl. Add sliced strawberries. Chill. When ready to serve, pour Dressing over salad. Toss gently.
Delicious and pretty!

Dressing:
1/4 C. lime juice
1/4 C. lemon juice
3 T. honey
2 T. olive oil

Combine and mix well.
Note: You may substitute 1 1/2 cups of Mandarin oranges for strawberries.

SUMMER SALAD

1 1/2 C. chopped cucumber
1/2 C. chopped green onion
1/2 C. diced celery
1/2 C. grated raw carrot

Mix all together. Chill and serve on lettuce with French dressing and crisp crackers.

TWENTY-FOUR HOUR VEGETABLE SALAD

1/2 lb. cooked bacon, broken
1 C. raw cauliflower
1 head lettuce, chopped
1/3 C. sugar
1/2 C. mayonnaise
1/3 C. Parmesan cheese
1 grated onion

Combine all ingredients. Let set in refrigerator overnight. Toss and serve.

- MAIN DISH SALADS -

DINNER IN A BOWL

1 lb. cooked chicken or turkey,
    diced or cut into julienne strips
1 tsp. salt
3 T. olive oil
1 tsp. paprika
1 tsp. thyme
1/2 tsp. garlic pepper
1/2 tsp. lemon pepper
1 clove garlic, peel and
    rub salad bowl with this
4 C. lettuce or any green leafy
    vegetable that does not
    require cooking
1 Bermuda onion, sliced and
    separated into rings
3 hard-boiled eggs, cut in slices
1/2 C. crumbled blue cheese or
    1 C. shredded Cheddar cheese
Salad dressing of choice

Combine all ingredients. Chill. Serve in large glass or wooden bowl. Serves 6 to 8.

FRUIT 'N CHICKEN SALAD

4 C. cooked chicken breast, diced
1 C. unpeeled apple, diced
1 C. celery, finely sliced
1 C. pineapple bits, drained
1 C. seedless green grapes, halved
1/2 to 3/4 C. Hellmann's mayonnaise
1/2 C. sliced almonds, toasted,
    for garnish
Lettuce leaves

In a large bowl, combine all ingredients, mixing gently. Use just enough mayonnaise to hold ingredients together. Chill. Serve on lettuce leaves and top with toasted almonds. Makes 10 to 12 servings.

SALMON SALAD

1 1-lb. can salmon
1 C. chopped celery
1 chopped green pepper
Mayonnaise

Remove skin and bones from fish. Flake fish; add the celery and pepper. Add mayonnaise to moisten. Serve on lettuce, with more dressing. Garnish with radishes, tomato wedges or olives.

SEAFOOD PASTA SALAD

Salad:
1 8-oz. bx. sea shell macaroni
1 8-oz. bx. tri-color twist macaroni
2 6-oz. cans crab meat, drained
2 C. boiled shrimp, diced or
    2 cans shrimp, drained
1 6-oz. can black olives, sliced
1 3-oz. bot. stuffed green olives
1 med. onion, chopped (optional)

Cook and drain sea shell and tri-color macaroni. Combine the macaroni with remaining salad ingredients. Pour the Dressing over mixture and mix gently. Chill. Serves 8 to 10.

Dressing:
1 1/2 C. Hellmann's mayonnaise
4 T. original Ranch dressing
4 T. milk
Salt and pepper, to taste
1/4 tsp. celery seeds

Combine ingredients.

Sylvia Herring McCurry
(Wife of Don McCurry,
One of the Twelve)
Lincolnton, GA

SHRIMP SALAD

1 head lettuce, washed and
    drained well
2 tomatoes, cut in small wedges
4 green onions, sliced thinly
4 radishes, slice thinly
2 cans med. shrimp, drained well
Hellmann's mayonnaise

In a large bowl with a tight-fitting cover, combine lettuce (cut in bite-size pieces), tomatoes, onions, radishes and shrimp. Mix. Cover and refrigerate for a few hours. Just before serving, add enough mayonnaise to moisten salad. Start with 1/2 cup and add whatever is needed. Toss and heap into salad bowls.

TUNA SALAD

2 6-oz. cans white Albacore tuna,
    drained
2 eggs, boiled and mashed fine
1/4 tsp. celery seed
2 T. sweet pickle relish
1 sm. onion, grated
1/2 tsp. lemon pepper
1/2 C. mayonnaise
1/8 tsp. salt
1/8 tsp. freshly ground pepper

Combine ingredients in a bowl. Mix well. Chill. Serve on leaves of lettuce or make sandwiches on plain or toasted bread spread lightly with mayonnaise.

- SALAD DRESSINGS -

BUTTERMILK DRESSING

1 C. Hellmann's mayonnaise
1 C. catsup
2 C. buttermilk
Salt and pepper, to taste
2 tsp. minced garlic

Mix all ingredients well. Refrigerate in covered container. Serve as a dressing for green salad.

CLASSIC FRENCH DRESSING

1 clove garlic
12 T. olive oil
2 tsp. salt
2 tsp. chili powder
4 T. wine vinegar

Crush garlic in a little of the oil. Remove garlic. Pour the oil, salt, chili powder and remaining olive oil into a bowl. Stir well. Then slowly add vinegar (pour in a thin stream). Stir well. Serve over tossed salad.

RUSSIAN DRESSING

1 C. mayonnaise
1 T. prepared horseradish
1/4 C. catsup or chili sauce
1 tsp. finely grated onion

Combine all ingredients. Cover; refrigerate. Makes 1 1/4 cups.

SWEET & SOUR DRESSING

1 clove garlic, minced
1 med. onion, minced
1 C. salad or olive oil
1/3 C. vinegar
1/2 C. catsup
1 tsp. Worcestershire sauce
1/2 C. sugar
1 tsp. salt

Mix all ingredients together. Beat with electric mixer or blend in blender a few seconds. Store in a pint jar. Shake well before serving. Makes 1 pint.
Good on green salads.

HOT VINAIGRETTE DRESSING

1 C. cider vinegar
1 C. light brown sugar
2 pieces bacon, cooked
   crisp and crumbled

Combine vinegar and sugar in a small saucepan. Cook until thin syrup consistency. Remove from heat. Add cooked, crumbled bacon. Serve hot over spinach salad with mushrooms.

- PRESERVING -

AUNT GLENNIE'S PEAR RELISH

1 pk. pears
6 red sweet peppers
6 green sweet peppers
8 hot peppers
6 onions
1 T. salt
1 T. celery seed
5 C. sugar
5 C. vinegar

Grind pears, peppers and onions. Add salt, celery seed, sugar and vinegar and boil 30 minutes. Stir constantly. Seal in jars. Makes 6 quarts.

Good with poultry or pork.

Glennie McCurry Norman
(One of the Twelve)
Thomson, GA

NANNIE'S GREEN TOMATO PICKLE

1 gal. green tomatoes
1/2 doz. lg. onions
1/2 C. salt
3 C. granulated sugar
1/2 lemon
3 pods red pepper
3 C. white vinegar
1 T. whole black peppercorns*
1 T. whole cloves*
1 T. celery seed*
1 T. mustard seed*
1 T. ground mustard*

*Tie in a square of cheesecloth.

Slice tomatoes and onions. Then sprinkle with salt. Let stand overnight. Drain well. Add lemon and pepper to vinegar. Add tomatoes and onions. Add spices (tied in cloth) and cook for 1/2 hour. Stir to prevent sticking. Pour in sterilized jars, seal and process according to canning directions.

Nannie was the mother of the Twelve.

Joann McCurry Ferguson
(One of the Twelve)
Lincolnton, GA

Breads,
Grits & Rice
Pasta

- BISCUITS -

AUNT JOANN'S BISCUITS

2 C. flour, sifted (all-purpose)
3 tsp. baking powder
1/4 tsp. baking soda
1 tsp. salt
4 T. shortening
2/3 C. buttermilk

Sift together flour, baking powder, soda and salt. Cut in shortening with a pastry blender until mixture looks like grains of rice. Add milk; stir quickly with a fork just enough to make a soft dough. Place dough on a floured surface and knead gently 6 to 8 times, forming a ball. Roll dough out to 1/2 to 3/4" thickness and cut with a biscuit cutter dipped in flour. Bake on an ungreased baking sheet at 450° for 12 to 15 minutes, until golden brown. Makes 12 to 15.

Joann McCurry Ferguson
(One of the Twelve)
Lincolnton, GA

AUNT PATSY'S BISCUITS

2 C. self-rising flour
1 stick butter, room temperature
1 C. buttermilk

Cut butter into flour with pastry cutter. Add buttermilk, stirring with spoon until well mixed; will be sticky. Knead dough gently on wax paper sprinkled with flour. Roll out to 1/2" thickness. Cut with biscuit cutter. Place on ungreased cookie sheet. Bake at 400° until brown.

Patsy McCurry Partridge
Lincolnton, GA

AUNT SYLVIA'S BISCUITS

3 1/2 C. self-rising flour
1/2 tsp. salt
2 tsp. baking powder
1/2 tsp. baking soda
3/4 C. lard
1 C. plus 2 T. buttermilk
1 C. sugar
1/2 C. water

Sift flour, salt, baking powder and soda together into a large bowl. Cut in lard with a pastry blender. Add buttermilk all at once. Then add sugar and water. Mix with your fingers until a soft dough forms. Turn out onto lightly floured surface. Dust top lightly with flour. Pat out dough so that it looks like a thick, round cake. Dip your hands in flour and knead the dough for 1 minute (fold outer edges to center overlapping and knead gently). Dust rolling pin with flour and roll dough 1/2" thick. Cut with a floured biscuit cutter (press cutter straight down and cut biscuits as close together as possible). Bake 1/2" apart on a greased cookie sheet. Preheat oven to 450°. Bake for 13 minutes. Serve hot. Makes 20.

Sylvia Herring McCurry
(Wife of Don McCurry,
One of the Twelve)
Lincolnton, GA

BISCUITS

1 3/4 C. sifted flour
1 tsp. salt
2 T. baking powder
6 T. very cold butter,
    cut in small pieces
2/3 C. milk

Sift flour, salt and baking powder together into a large bowl. Cut in the butter until consistency of cornmeal. Pour milk into mixture and stir with a knife until dough is together. Turn out onto a floured surface. Knead gently for about 1/2 minute. Roll or pat dough to 1/2" thickness. Cut with a biscuit cutter. Bake on greased cookie sheet at 450° for 12 to 14 minutes. Makes 1 dozen.

BUTTERMILK BISCUITS

1 3/4 C. all-purpose flour, sifted
1 tsp. salt
3 tsp. baking powder
1 tsp. sugar
1/2 tsp. baking soda
5 T. butter
2/3 to 3/4 C. buttermilk

Sift flour before measuring. Add other dry ingredients and then sift again. Cut in butter. Add milk to form a soft dough. Pat out on a floured board to 1/2" thickness. Cut out and arrange on an ungreased baking sheet. Bake for 12 to 15 minutes at 450°. Makes 2 dozen biscuits, about 1 1/2" wide.

FRIED BISCUITS (USED AS HUSHPUPPIES)

2 cans refrigerated biscuits
   (the least expensive ones
   are best)
Oil, for frying

Open the biscuits and drop one by one into very hot oil in heavy skillet at least 2½ to 3" deep. Biscuits will puff up. When bottoms are brown, turn them over in oil and brown on other side. Drain on paper towels. Serve hot. Makes 20 servings.

Wonderful when you punch a hole in the top and fill it with honey. Very good with fried fish.

ROLLED BISCUIT DOUGH

2 C. all-purpose flour
1/2 tsp. salt
4 tsp. baking powder
1/2 tsp. cream of tartar
2 tsp. sugar
1/2 C. margarine or shortening
2/3 C. milk (buttermilk is best)

Sift dry ingredients into a large mixing bowl. Cut in shortening until mixture is crumbly. Add milk. Roll out to 1/2" thickness on a floured surface. Cut with a biscuit cutter or a glass (rim dipped in flour first). Bake on an ungreased baking pan or in an iron skillet at 450° for 10 to 12 minutes. Makes 1 dozen.

SOUR CREAM BISCUITS

2 C. all-purpose flour
1 T. baking powder
1/2 tsp. baking soda
1 tsp. salt
1 C. sour cream
1/4 C. milk

Sift dry ingredients together into a mixing bowl. Fold in sour cream; stir in milk until dough is soft. Knead on floured surface. Pat or roll out to 1/2" thickness. Cut with biscuit cutter dipped in flour. Bake on greased cookie sheet at 450° for 10 minutes. Makes 1 dozen.

SOUTHERN BISCUITS

2 C. plain flour
4 tsp. baking powder
1 tsp. salt
1/2 tsp. baking soda
1/4 C. shortening equals 4 T. Crisco
1 C. buttermilk

Preheat oven to 475°. Sift flour, baking powder, salt and baking soda into a large bowl, cut the shortening in with a pastry cutter. Add the buttermilk gradually. Stir with a knife until well blended. Turn dough out on a floured surface. Knead very gently until smooth, about 1/2 minute (flour your hands). Bake on greased cookie sheet in preheated oven for 12 minutes. Makes 16 to 18 (2") biscuits.

SWEET POTATO BISCUITS

1 C. mashed sweet potatoes, cooked
1/3 C. melted butter
1 beaten egg
1 C. sifted flour
2 tsp. baking powder
1/2 tsp. salt

Combine sweet potatoes, butter and beaten egg. Sift flour, baking powder and salt together. Blend into potato mixture. Drop by scant tablespoonfuls onto greased baking sheet. Bake at 400° for 12 to 15 minutes. Serve hot with butter. Makes 8 to 10 biscuits.

TIPSY ANGELS (ANGEL BISCUITS)

1 20-oz. pkg. Bisquick mix
1 can beer, room temperature
2 T. sugar

Mix and let stand for 30 minutes. Spoon into greased muffin tin. Bake at 375° for 20 minutes or at 425° for 10 minutes.

- BREADS -

APPLE BREAD

1 stick margarine
1 C. sugar
1 egg
2 C. flour
1 tsp. baking soda
1/2 tsp. salt
1/2 tsp. ground cloves
1 tsp. cinnamon
2 C. pared, chopped apples
2/3 C. nuts
Raisins (optional)

Cream margarine and sugar. Add egg and beat. Sift together dry ingredients and add. Stir in apples, nuts and raisins. Dough will be stiff! Bake in 1 large or 2 small greased and floured pans at 350° for 1 hour or less for 2 small pans.

LEMON BREAD

2/3 C. margarine
1 1/4 C. sugar
2 eggs
Grated rind and juice of 1 lg. lemon
1 1/2 C. flour
2 tsp. baking powder
1/2 tsp. salt
1/2 C. milk
1/2 C. nuts

Cream margarine and sugar; add eggs and lemon. Sift dry ingredients; add alternately with milk; add nuts. Pour into 9x5" greased and floured pan. Let rise a few minutes. Bake at 350° for 50 to 60 minutes. Take out and pour Glaze over.

Glaze:
1/2 stick margarine
1/2 C. sugar
Juice and rind of 1 lemon

Combine ingredients and cook over low heat until thick.

NUT BREAD

3 C. all-purpose flour
1 C. granulated sugar
1 C. milk
2 C. chopped nuts
3 tsp. baking powder
1 tsp. salt
1 egg, beaten

Beat egg; add sugar gradually. Combine baking powder and salt with flour. Add flour mixture alternately with milk until used. Add nuts. Stir and pour into a loaf pan which has been greased or sprayed with Baker's Joy. Bake at 350° for 50 to 60 minutes. Slice and serve.

Lovely toasted, topped with whipped cream.

BROTHER'S ZUCCHINI BREAD

3 eggs
1 C. vegetable oil
2 C. granulated sugar
2 C. all-purpose flour
2 C. shredded zucchini
1 C. chopped nuts (pecans or walnuts)
1/4 tsp. baking powder
1 tsp. salt
2 tsp. soda
2 tsp. vanilla
2 tsp. ground cinnamon

Combine all ingredients in a large bowl. Stir. Pour into 2 greased and floured loaf pans. Bake at 350° for 1 hour. Cool. Slice and spread with softened cream cheese. Makes 2 loaves.

Note: Strawberry preserves may be added to cream cheese.

Allen & Marguerite McCurry
(Allen is One of the Twelve)
Gainesville, GA

BEER BATTER BREAD

3 C. self-rising flour
3 T. sugar
1 can beer (regular size - any kind)

Combine ingredients in a large mixing bowl; mix well. Pour into greased loaf pan. Bake at 350° for 1 hour. Makes 12 servings.

Good and easy!

EASY CHEESY BREAD

2 1/2 C. Bisquick (or other biscuit mix)
1 C. shredded extra sharp
   Cheddar cheese
2 tsp. poppy seeds
1 lg. egg, beaten
1 C. milk
Few grains cayenne pepper

Combine biscuit mix, cheese and poppy seeds in a large mixing bowl. In a separate bowl, mix egg, milk and cayenne. Pour into biscuit mix. Stir until well blended. Pour mixture into a greased loaf pan and bake at 350° for 30 to 35 minutes. Serve hot or cooled. Makes 1 loaf.

GRANNIE'S EGG BREAD

1 C. sifted plain cornmeal
1 C. buttermilk
1 egg, beaten
2 T. shortening, melted
1 tsp. baking powder
1/2 tsp. soda
1/2 tsp. salt

Mix ingredients in order listed. Stir until well blended. Grease a cast iron cornstick or muffin pan with shortening. Heat in 400° oven. Pour mix into heated pans and bake for 20 minutes or until lightly browned on top.

Grace Booker Radford
Dawson, GA

GARLIC BREAD

1 loaf French bread, cut
　in 1" thick slices
1/2 C. butter
1 clove garlic, minced

Combine butter and garlic. Place bread on a large piece of foil; slice on the diagonal, not quite through to the bottom so that loaf stays together. Spread with garlic butter and cover, leaving foil open at the top. Bake at 375° for 10 to 20 minutes.

POPOVERS

2 C. sifted plain flour
2 tsp. salt
2 eggs
2 C. milk

Beat eggs until frothy; add flour, sifted with salt, and 1 cup of the milk. Beat mixture until well blended, then add remaining milk and beat again until smooth. Chill batter in refrigerator. Grease a muffin tin (preferably an iron one) with unsalted vegetable shortening and heat to sizzling point. Pour in batter and bake at 450° for 15 minutes, then at 350° for 20 minutes. Makes 8 to 10 servings.

PUFFY DUMPLINGS

1 C. flour
2 tsp. baking powder
1/4 tsp. salt
1/8 tsp. pepper
1/2 C. milk
Broth*

*May be used for chicken and dumplings by first cooking a chicken in a large saucepan half filled with water and seasoned with salt. Remove bones from chicken, etc.

Combine all ingredients, adding milk last. Stir until smooth. Drop from a teaspoon into broth of choice. Cover and boil 5 to 7 minutes. Do not uncover while cooking.

JIFFY ROLLS

2 C. self-rising flour
1/4 C. sugar
1/4 C. shortening, melted (Crisco)
3/4 C. warm water
1 pkg. yeast, dissolved
   in 1/2 T. hot water

Combine all ingredients. Mix well and put equal amounts into a well-greased muffin tin. Bake at 400° for 15 minutes. Makes 1 dozen.
Good!

TOAST POINTS

1 loaf day old bread (thin sliced)
1 stick melted butter or margarine

Trim crusts from each slice. Cut in half (diagonally). Brush both sides lightly with melted butter. Place on baking sheet. Bake at 300° for 20 to 25 minutes or until crisp and lightly browned.

- CORNBREADS -

BROCCOLI CORNBREAD

4 eggs, beaten
1 10-oz. pkg. frozen, chopped
   broccoli (uncooked)
1 med. onion, minced fine
1 6-oz. ctn. cottage cheese
1 stick margarine, melted
3/4 tsp. salt
1 bx. Jiffy cornbread mix

In a mixing bowl, beat eggs; add broccoli, cottage cheese, melted margarine, salt, onions and cornbread mix. Pour into greased 9x13" baking dish or in muffin tins. Bake at 400° for 25 to 30 minutes. Makes 36 (8 to 10 servings).

CORN STICKS

2 C. yellow cornmeal
1 C. all-purpose flour
1/4 C. sugar
1 T. baking powder
1 tsp. salt
1/2 tsp. baking soda
2 eggs, lightly beaten
2 C. buttermilk
6 T. butter, melted

Preheat oven to hot (425°). Lightly grease cornstick pan. Place in oven to warm while preparing batter. Combine cornmeal, flour, sugar, baking powder, salt and baking soda in large bowl. Add eggs, buttermilk and butter; stir just to moisten. Pour batter into each cornstick mold, filling each about 3/4 full. Bake in preheated oven for about 15 minutes or until tops are lightly browned. Cool in pan on wire rack for 10 minutes.

CRACKLIN' BREAD

1 C. cornmeal
2 C. flour
1 1/4 tsp. salt
4 1/2 tsp. baking powder
4 T. sugar
1/2 C. cracklings
1 lg. egg, beaten
1 1/2 C. milk
4 T. melted shortening or
    bacon drippings

Preheat oven to 400°. Pour 1 tablespoon oil in black iron skillet. Place in oven to heat. In a bowl, combine flour, cornmeal, salt, baking powder, sugar, and cracklings. Beat egg, milk and shortening together. Add to dry ingredients. Mix well; pour into heated skillet. Bake at 400° for 35 to 40 minutes. Slice in wedges.

Good with turnip greens or collards.

OLD FASHIONED HOE CAKE

2 heaping T. self-rising cornmeal
1 heaping T. self-rising flour
1/4 C. water
3 T. very hot cooking oil or
    bacon drippings

Mix cornmeal, flour and water in a bowl and pour mixture into an iron frying pan in which oil or drippings have been heated. Cook on one side until edges are brown, turn and cook until browned on other side. Serves 2.

Perfect with collard greens or just about anything else! Great with syrup too!

Note: This was first cooked over hot coals on the blade of a hoe several hundred years ago.

HUSHPUPPIES

1 1/2 C. cornmeal
1 1/2 C. water
1 T. vegetable oil
2 tsp. salt
1 med. onion, grated
2 lg. eggs, beaten
3 tsp. baking powder
1 tsp. granulated sugar
A few grains of cayenne pepper

In a saucepan, cook cornmeal and water until stiff. Remove from heat. Add remaining ingredients in order listed. Drop by teaspoonfuls into hot oil. Fry until they're golden brown. Turn once while frying. Drain on paper towels. Serve hot with fish or seafood. Makes 2 to 2 1/2 dozen.

Southern folklore has it that Hushpuppies originated in a kitchen where some hunters were eating and their hunting dogs were under the table whining. The hunters would feed them cornbread and say "Oh, hush puppy."

SOUTHERN CORNBREAD

1 C. yellow cornmeal
1 C. flour
3 tsp. baking powder
1/2 tsp. salt
1/4 C. sugar
1 C. milk
1/4 C. melted butter
1 beaten egg

Sift cornmeal, flour, baking powder, salt and sugar. Stir in milk, butter and beaten egg. Bake in a well-greased, heated, black cast iron skillet or any baking dish or muffin tin at 425° for 20 to 25 minutes. Makes 8 servings.

SOUTHERN SPOON BREAD

3/4 C. plain cornmeal
1 tsp. salt
3 T. melted butter or margarine
1 C. boiling water
1 C. milk
2 eggs, well beaten
2 tsp. baking powder

Combine meal, salt and butter in mixing bowl. Add boiling water slowly and beat with a spoon until smooth. Add milk, eggs and baking powder. Mix thoroughly. Pour into heated, well-greased iron skillet. Bake at 350° for 45 minutes.

Grace Booker Radford
Dawson, GA

- MUFFINS -

MAYO MUFFINS

2 C. all-purpose flour
2 tsp. baking powder
1/2 tsp. salt
1/2 C. mayonnaise
3/4 C. milk

Mix first 3 ingredients in a small bowl. Fold in mayonnaise and milk. Stir until dough is moistened. Lightly butter muffin pans and fill each muffin cup 3/4 full. Bake at 450° in preheated oven for 10 to 12 minutes. Makes 8 muffins.
Note: For cheese muffins, add 1/2 cup grated cheese.

SOUR CREAM MUFFINS

2 C. self-rising flour
8 oz. (1 C.) sour cream
2 sticks butter, melted

Mix together. Spray small tins with Pam. Fill 2/3 full. Bake at 375° for 20 minutes. Makes 2 1/2 dozen.

Lynda Rogers
Manchester, GA

- BUTTERS -

HOMEMADE BUTTER

1 lb. margarine, softened
1 C. buttermilk
3/4 C. cooking oil

With an electric mixer, mix all ingredients together until well blended. Mold into shape desired and refrigerate until ready to use. Makes 2 pounds.
Scrumptious!

HONEY BUTTER

1/2 C. light honey
1/2 C. butter, softened

Mix well. Chill and serve with fresh baked bread or spread on toast.
If you want a larger quantity, just mix equal parts of honey and butter.

TOMATO BUTTER

3/4 C. butter, softened
1/2 tsp. salt
1/2 tsp. basil
Generous dash of pepper
3 firm tomatoes, peeled and chopped

Combine first 3 ingredients. Set aside. Peel tomatoes, chop fine and strain through a sieve. Drain on paper towels for 5 minutes. Add to butter mixture, stirring well to blend.
Wonderful on biscuits or cornbread.

- GRITS -

CONFEDERATE PUDDING

1 qt. boiling grits
1 egg, beaten
1 C. milk
Salt, to taste

Beat ingredients together; bake in a hot 375 to 400° oven for 40 minutes. Serves 6 to 8.
Good and easy.

FRIED GRITS

2 C. cooked grits (cold)
3 eggs, beaten
Salt and pepper, to taste
1/4 tsp. Tabasco sauce
1/4 tsp. sugar
Oil, for frying

In a shallow bowl, mash grits (use a potato masher or a fork) until small grains like rice. Add eggs, salt, pepper, Tabasco and sugar. Mix well. Put 1/2" of oil in a heavy skillet, over medium/high heat until hot. Drop grits mixture by heaping tablespoonfuls into oil. Brown lightly on both sides. Best when served right away. Makes 6 to 8 servings.

Note: Add more oil if needed with frying.

GARLIC GRITS

2 C. cooked grits
2 eggs, beaten
1/3 C. milk
1 tsp. salt
1 stick garlic cheese
1 stick butter

Combine grits, eggs, milk and salt. Melt cheese and butter in a saucepan over low heat. Remove from heat and stir in grits mixture. Pour into a buttered 9x9" casserole dish. Bake at 350° for 30 minutes. Makes 6 servings.

GRITS PUDDING

1 1/2 C. grits (white or yellow)
6 C. water
2 sticks butter or margarine
8 oz. grated sharp Cheddar cheese
3 eggs, beaten lightly
4 tsp. seasoning salt
Cayenne pepper and Tabasco sauce

Cook grits with water in large pot until thick. Add remaining ingredients. Bake in buttered 9x13" casserole dish for 1½ hours at 350°. Serve hot! Makes 8 servings.

Betty Miller Wilkins
Prosperity, SC

TOMATO CHEESE GRITS

1 16-oz. bx. yellow or white grits,
    cooked according to directions
2 #2 cans stewed tomatoes, chopped
1 lb. extra sharp Cheddar cheese,
    grated
1 stick butter
2 T. sugar
1 tsp. Tabasco sauce (or more
    if you like it hot)

Drain tomatoes; reserve liquid. In a large pot, cook grits according to package directions (using tomato liquid for part of water). During last few minutes of cooking, stir in chopped tomatoes, cheese, butter, sugar and Tabasco sauce. Serves a crowd.

Wonderful with fried fish and fried canned biscuits.

- RICE -

AUNT WARDELL'S PARTY PAELLA

1/4 C. olive oil
6 chicken breasts
2 lb. med. shrimp, shelled, tails intact
1 med. onion, chopped
1 lg. green bell pepper, diced
2 lb. boneless pork chops
4 cloves garlic, minced
1 bay leaf
1/2 tsp. saffron threads
Lg. pinch dried thyme
1 35-oz. can Italian plum tomatoes,
    coarsely broken up in colander
    and drained well
Salt and freshly ground pepper
2 C. (about 1-lb.) Italian short-grain
    rice (Arborio or Tesori) or
    Uncle Ben's long-grain rice
2 (13 3/4-oz.) cans chicken broth
1 (6 1/2-oz.) jar whole pimiento or
    roasted peppers, drained, diced
1/2 C. frozen peas
6 sm. mussels, soaked,
    scrubbed, and bearded
12 to 16 stuffed Spanish olives

Heat oil in deep ovenproof 12" skillet or paella pan over medium-high heat. Add chicken and saute, turning all pieces once or twice, until light golden, about 12 minutes. Transfer to plate. Add shrimp to skillet and cook, tossing frequently, 1 minute. Transfer to plate. Add onion and bell pepper to skillet. Reduce heat to medium and cook, stirring frequently, until slightly softened, about 10 minutes. Stir in pork chops, garlic, bay leaf, saffron, and thyme; cook 4 minutes. Stir in tomatoes and pinch each of salt and pepper. Cook, stirring and breaking up tomatoes, about 5 minutes. Heat oven to 350°. Add rice to skillet and stir with large fork until grains are translucent, about 5 minutes. Pour broth into quart measure, spoon off fat, and add enough cold water to make 1 quart. Pour diluted broth into skillet and increase heat slightly. Heat to boiling, then gently boil 5 minutes, stirring frequently. Remove from heat. Tuck chicken and shrimp into rice. Scatter pimiento and peas over top. Bake uncovered until liquid is absorbed but rice is still moist, about 15 minutes. Add mussels and bake 5 minutes longer. Remove skillet from oven and cover tightly with foil. Let stand 5 minutes. Scatter olives over paella and serve hot.

Wardell McCurry Briceño
(One of the Twelve)
Jonesboro, GA

BAKED RICE AND MUSHROOMS

2 med. onions, peeled and
    sliced 1/4" thick
1 8-oz. can sliced mushrooms, drained
1 stick butter or margarine
1 can consomme
1 C. water
1 C. uncooked rice
1 T. dried parsley

Place butter in skillet and saute onions and mushrooms for 45 minutes on medium/high heat. Add rice and parsley. Stir and pour into buttered 9x13" casserole dish. Cover with foil and bake at 350° for 45 to 50 minutes. Makes 4 to 6 servings.

BETH'S BROWN RICE

2 C. Minute rice (uncooked)
1/2 tsp. salt
1 pkg. dried onion soup mix
1/2 med. onion, chopped
1 stick margarine
2 C. water

Saute onion in melted butter; add remaining ingredients. Pour in buttered casserole dish. Bake at 350° until water is absorbed.

Beth Radford Ashmore
Lincolnton, GA

BROCCOLI AND RICE CASSEROLE

1 C. Minute rice (cooked)
1 pkg. chopped broccoli
1/2 C. celery
1/2 C. onion
1 can cream of mushroom soup
1 8-oz. jar Cheez Whiz

Cook Minute rice and broccoli according to directions on packages. After cooking rice and broccoli, combine with remaining ingredients. Add salt and pepper to taste. Bake at 350° for 35 to 40 minutes.

Can be cooked in microwave in half the time.

Lynda Rogers
Manchester, GA

CHICKEN AND RICE CASSEROLE

1 C. uncooked rice
4 chicken breast halves
1 can cream of chicken soup
1 soup can of water
1/2 C. melted butter
1 T. chopped onion
1/2 tsp. salt
1/4 tsp. pepper
1/2 tsp. dried tarragon
1/4 tsp. paprika

Spread rice on bottom of 9x13" baking dish. Arrange chicken breasts, skin side up, over rice. Mix soup, water and seasonings together and pour over chicken. Bake at 350° for 1½ hours covered with foil. Makes 4 servings.

PARSLEY RICE

1 C. raw long grain rice,
    cooked and cooled
1/2 tsp. salt
1 bunch parsley (30 sprigs)
4 green onions
2 tsp. dry minced onion
1/4 lb. butter or margarine
1/4 lb. grated American cheese
1/2 pt. table cream
    (evaporated milk)
Additional chopped parsley,
    for garnish

Cook rice. Cool. Chop parsley (finely), green onion and dry onions. Add to rice and mix thoroughly. Layer in a 9x9" casserole dish: rice mixture first, then layer of cheese, dotted with butter. Repeat. Pour 1/4 cup cream over top. Bake at 400° until cheese browns on top; then reduce heat to 300°. Pour remaining cream over top. Bake for 30 minutes. Sprinkle chopped parsley over top when ready to serve. Serve hot. Makes 4 servings.

PARTY RICE

1 C. long grain rice
  (Uncle Ben's brand)
1 1/2 C. water
1/2 C. dry white wine
1 env. golden onion soup mix
1/2 C. chopped celery
2 T. butter
1 tsp. salt
1/2 tsp. white pepper
1/4 C. or more slivered almonds

Brown rice and almonds in butter. Add remaining ingredients. Cover and cook over low heat until rice is done.

Note: For individual servings, pack cooked party rice in a small ring mold and invert on plate. Very good with Chicken Magnolia (see Table of Contents).

Flo Pursley
Lincolnton, GA

PORCUPINES

1 lb. lean ground beef
1 C. uncooked long-grain rice
1 med. onion, minced
1 #2 can tomatoes, mashed smooth
1 T. minute tapioca
Salt and pepper, to taste
1/2 tsp. dried basil

In a mixing bowl, combine beef, rice, onions, salt and pepper. Shape into 4 balls. Place in a glass baking dish. Mix mashed tomatoes with basil and tapioca. Pour over "porcupine" balls. Cover and bake at 350° for 30 minutes. Makes 4 servings.

RED BEANS AND RICE

1 15-oz. pkg. red beans
1 pkg. bacon (or fat meat)
Uncooked rice (see below for amount)*
1 lg. onion

No pre-soaking needed. Fry 6 to 9 slices of bacon or fat meat. Set aside. Place red beans in large pot with onions and bacon drippings. Fill completely with water. Season to taste. Cover and cook slowly so that gravy can thicken. Let simmer for 1 hour and 15 minutes. Add bacon (crumbled) and uncooked rice. Stir well. Let simmer for 20 minutes.

Serve with salad, French bread, and a pitcher of iced tea and you'll have a great meal!
  *1 cup gravy - 1/2 cup rice.
  *2 cups gravy - 1 cup rice.
  *3 cups gravy - 1 1/2 cups rice.

SAUSAGE AND RICE DINNER

2 lb. Jimmy Dean hot sausage (bulk)*
1 lg. onion, chopped
2 C. uncooked rice
1 1/2 C. celery, chopped
2 1/2 tsp. salt
1/4 tsp. black pepper
2 1/2 C. water

*Two pounds of ground beef may be substituted.

Make sausage into very small balls and cook until lightly browned (10 to 12 minutes). Remove and drain on paper towels. Discard all but 3 tablespoons of drippings from sausage. Add onion and rice and cook in the drippings until browned lightly. Add sausage, celery, seasonings and water. Cover; reduce heat and simmer 40 minutes or until all liquid is absorbed. Stir during cooking once or twice. Makes 10 servings.

If you wish, this can be made ahead, cooked for 20 minutes, then refrigerated and cooked for 30 minutes more before serving.

SAVANNAH SAUSAGE AND RICE

1 C. raw rice (long-grain)
1 lb. loose, hot sausage, browned and drained
1 can onion soup
1 can beef broth or consomme

Place cooked and drained sausage in bottom of casserole dish. Pour raw rice over sausage. Pour soups over top. Bake at 350° for 1 hour. Serve hot. Makes 4 servings.

SKILLET SPANISH RICE

1/4 C. Wesson oil
1 med. onion, thinly sliced
1/2 med. green pepper, chopped
1 C. regular rice (uncooked)
1/2 lb. ground beef
2 8-oz. cans tomato sauce
1 3/4 C. hot water
1 tsp. prepared mustard (optional)
1 tsp. salt
Dash pepper

Heat oil in skillet. Add onion, green pepper, rice and beef. Stir over high heat until lightly browned. Add tomato sauce and remaining ingredients. Mix well. Bring quickly to a boil. Cover tightly and simmer for 25 minutes. Makes 4 servings.

Betty Miller Wilkins
Prosperity, SC

TERESA'S BROWN RICE

1/2 stick butter or margarine
1 C. French onion soup
1 C. beef consomme
1 C. raw Uncle Ben's rice

Melt butter in casserole dish. Combine remaining ingredients. Pour over melted butter. Bake at 375° for 1 hour or less. Serves 4.

Teresa McCurry Tankersley
Lincolnton, GA

- PASTAS -

BACON/MACARONI CASSEROLE

2 C. elbow macaroni,
    cooked and drained
1 lb. bacon
1/2 C. chopped onion
1 C. grated sharp Cheddar cheese
1 can tomato soup or
    1 can stewed tomatoes
1 C. milk

Set cooked and drained macaroni aside. Cut all but 4 slices of bacon into 1/2" crosswise slices. Fry the small pieces of bacon. Remove bacon from skillet; set aside. Saute onions in bacon drippings until soft. Remove onions from bacon drippings. Combine cooked bacon, macaroni, onion, cheese, soup (or tomatoes) and milk. Pour into buttered baking dish. Place the 4 uncooked slices of bacon on top. Bake at 375° for 30 minutes. Cool 5 minutes before serving. Serves 6.

BUTTONS AND BOWS

8 oz. bow tie macaroni
    (med.-size farfalle)
2 C. Hellmann's mayonnaise
1/2 C. plus 2 T. buttermilk
2 T. lemon juice
2 T. Dijon mustard
1 T. granulated sugar
1 10-oz. pkg. frozen peas, thawed,
    uncooked, drained
1 10-oz. can button mushrooms, sliced
Salt and pepper, to taste
8 slices bacon, fried crisp
    and crumbled

Cook macaroni as per package directions. Rinse in cold water and drain. With a whisk or electric mixer, combine mayonnaise, buttermilk, lemon juice, mustard and sugar. Mix well. Pour into a large bowl. Add pasta, peas and mushrooms. Toss to coat. Salt and pepper to taste. Top with crumbled bacon. Chill and serve on lettuce leaves.

Side Dishes

APPLE AND ONION SAUTE

1/4 C. butter or margarine or
    butter-flavored Crisco
4 C. thinly sliced onions
4 C. apples, peeled and quartered
    (may use 2 C. red apples and
    2 C. green apples to equal 4 C.)
2 tsp. salt
2 T. sugar

Heat butter in a large skillet on medium heat. Add onions and apples. Cover and cook for 10 to 12 minutes. Stir a few times during cooking. When onions are slightly browned, add salt and sugar. Serve hot.

Unusual colorful, and delicious with ham or turkey.

ASPARAGUS CASSEROLE

2 15-oz. cans whole asparagus spears,
    drained
1 can cream of mushroom soup
1 4-oz. can sliced mushrooms
2 C. grated sharp Cheddar cheese
1 3-oz. can French fried onion rings

Place 1 can drained asparagus spears on bottom of buttered 9x13" casserole dish. Top with can of soup. Next, add mushrooms and 1 cup of cheese. Add second can of drained asparagus and top with remaining cheese. Bake at 350° for 30 minutes. Remove from oven, top with onion rings and bake for 5 minutes more. Serves 6.

Note: 1 cup of Ritz cracker crumbs instead of onions may be used. Add before baking time begins.

ROLLED ASPARAGUS SPEARS

1/4 lb. prosciutto ham,
    sliced wafer thin
1 can asparagus spears,
    drained well

Place each asparagus spear on the edge of a separate piece of ham. Roll ham slice around asparagus. Refrigerate until ready to serve.

Pretty on a bed of lettuce or spinach leaves.

BUTTER BEAN CASSEROLE (AKA LIMA BEANS)

2 10-oz. pkg. frozen baby lima beans,
    cooked as per pkg. directions
3/4 C. sour cream
2 T. sugar
1/4 C. butter or margarine
2 tsp. dry mustard
2 T. molasses

Combine cooked beans with remaining ingredients. Stir gently. Pour into a lightly buttered 9x13" casserole dish. Bake at 375° for 30 minutes.

AUNT SYLVIA'S GREEN BEANS

1 gal. Italian green beans
2 sm. ham hocks
3 qt. water
2 tsp. salt

Place ham hocks, water and salt in a large pot. Cover and boil for 30 minutes. Drain beans and add to water and ham hocks. Add enough water to cover the beans. Cover and simmer for 30 minutes. Remove ham hocks from the beans and serve beans in a large bowl. Makes 20 to 24 servings.

The best green beans you've ever tasted.

Sylvia Herring McCurry
(Wife of Don McCurry,
One of the Twelve)
Lincolnton, GA

GREEN BEAN CASSEROLE I

1 T. melted butter or margarine
2 16-oz. cans whole green beans,
    drained
1 can sliced water chestnuts, drained
1 10-oz. can cream of celery soup
1 3-oz. can chow mein noodles
1 1/2 C. sharp Cheddar cheese,
    shredded

Preheat oven to 325°. Combine first 4 ingredients. Put noodles and cheese on casserole just before baking. Bake for 45 minutes.

GREEN BEAN CASSEROLE II

2 10-oz. pkg. frozen green beans,
    cooked as per instructions
4 slices bacon, cooked and diced
2/3 C. finely chopped onion
1 T. all-purpose flour
1 T. granulated sugar
1/2 C. milk
1/4 C. mayonnaise
1/4 C. shredded sharp
    Cheddar cheese
1/2 C. buttered Ritz cracker crumbs

Drain cooked green beans. Set aside. Fry bacon pieces in a skillet until crisp. Remove bacon and drain. Saute onions in bacon drippings until tender; remove onion; set aside. To the bacon drippings, add flour and sugar and cook for 1 minute, stirring all the while. Add milk, cook and stir until thickened. Fold in mayonnaise, green beans, bacon and onion. Pour into buttered 9x13" casserole dish. Top with cheese and bread crumbs. Bake at 350° for 25 minutes. Let stand for 5 to 7 minutes before serving. Makes 6 servings.

SUCCOTASH

1 10-oz. pkg. frozen lima beans
   (Fordhooks)
1 10-oz. pkg. frozen whole kernel corn
Salt and pepper, to taste
1 T. cream
2 T. butter or margarine

Combine both packages of vegetables in a saucepan and cook as per directions. Add cream and butter.

A good traditional southern dish.

BEAUTIFUL BEETS

1 16-oz. can sliced beets, chilled
1/2 C. honey Dijon dressing
   (fat-free or regular flavor)

Open can of beets; pour juice out. Pour dressing over beets while they are still in the can. Let stand for 1 minute. Pour into glass serving dish; stir until beets are coated and dressing is "rose petal pink" colored. (No cooking is required.) Makes 6 servings.

This is a pretty dish to serve and tastes wonderful!

BAKED BROCCOLI

2 10-oz. pkg. chopped broccoli,
   cooked as per directions or
   1 lg. head fresh broccoli
1 T. butter, melted
1 C. mayonnaise
1 stick butter or margarine, softened
1 C. Half and Half
2 eggs, beaten
1 med. onion, chopped
1 tsp. salt
Dash pepper (freshly ground is best)
2 C. extra sharp Cheddar cheese,
   grated
2 C. cheese or Ritz crackers,
   finely crushed

Drain cooked broccoli. Combine in a large bowl, broccoli, butter, mayonnaise, Half and Half, eggs, onion, salt and pepper. Add 1 cup of the cheese and 1 1/2 cups cracker crumbs. Mix well. Pour into a buttered 9x13" casserole dish. Top with remaining cheese and cracker crumbs. Bake in preheated 350° oven for 30 to 40 minutes. Let stand 15 to 20 minutes before serving. Makes 8 servings.

BROCCOLI CASSEROLE

1 can cream of mushroom soup
1 C. sharp Cheddar cheese, grated
2 well-beaten eggs
1 C. mayonnaise
2 T. onion, grated
1 sm. jar pimiento
Salt
Pepper
2 10-oz. pkg. broccoli, chopped

Mix and pour over broccoli which has been cooked (half time) and drained. Top with buttered bread crumbs. Bake at 400° for 20 minutes.

Patsy McCurry Partridge
(One of the Twelve)
Lincolnton, GA

CREAMED CABBAGE

4 C. shredded green cabbage
8 C. water
2 tsp. salt
1 tsp. cornstarch
2 chicken bouillon cubes
1/4 C. boiling water
1 C. sour cream
1 tsp. dillweed

In a large saucepan, cook cabbage in water and salt until tender. Drain cabbage and set aside. Dissolve cornstarch and bouillon cubes in boiling water. Stir into cooked, drained cabbage. Fold in sour cream and dillweed. Serve hot. Makes 6 servings.

GLAZED CARROTS

1/2 C. orange marmalade
2 tsp. cornstarch
1 T. butter
2 T. slivered almonds
1 lb. carrots, sliced, cooked, drained

Combine marmalade and cornstarch in saucepan; add remaining ingredients. Simmer, stirring occasionally, until slightly thickened. Yield: 4 servings.

MAKE AHEAD CARROT CASSEROLE

8 lg. carrots, cooked in salted water
    until tender
Salt and pepper, to taste

Drain carrots. Reserve 2 tablespoons liquid. Place carrots in buttered 9x13" casserole dish. Sprinkle with salt and pepper to taste. Spread Sauce over carrots and top with Topping (bread crumbs). Bake at 350° for 30 minutes. Makes 8 servings.

May be cooked immediately or refrigerated and cooked the next day.

Sauce:
1 C. mayonnaise
2 T. horseradish
2 T. grated onion
2 T. carrot liquid
1 tsp. dried mint leaves (optional)

Combine ingredients.

Topping:
3/4 C. bread crumbs

CHEESE CASSEROLE

6 slices bread, with crusts removed
2 1/2 T. melted butter
Paprika
4 eggs, slightly beaten
2 1/2 C. milk
3/4 tsp. pepper
1 tsp. salt
1 tsp. dry mustard
1 1/4 C. shredded Cheddar cheese

Cut bread into rounds; brush with butter and sprinkle with paprika. Layer into a buttered 8" square baking dish. Combine remaining ingredients and pour into dish. Bake at 300° for 30 minutes, until center is firm. Yield: 6 servings.

Serve hot with ham.

SOUTHERN COLLARD GREENS

1 lg. bunch collard greens,
   washed and cut in pieces
1 ham hock
1 T. salt
2 tsp. Tabasco sauce
3 T. white or red wine
2 T. granulated sugar

Place 6 to 8 cups of water in a large pot with ham hock. Cover and boil for 30 minutes. Wash collard greens (leaf by leaf under running cold water and drain). Trim large stems out (use kitchen shears). Place several leaves at a time in a stack; fold in half and cut in 2" strips with scissors or kitchen shears until all are cut. Place collards in water with ham hocks. Bring to a boil. Add remaining ingredients and simmer covered until tender, adding just enough water to keep covered. Serves 6.

Collard greens will cook down to about a third of original volume so consider this when purchasing. Serve hot with hot pepper sauce.

Note: The wine will keep them from smelling so "strong".

BROILED CORN ON THE COB

6 ears of corn, husked and silked
2/3 C. smooth peanut butter
6 slices bacon

Coat each ear of corn liberally with peanut butter. Wrap each with slice of bacon. Secure ends of bacon with toothpicks. Broil. Turn several times until bacon is crisp. Serve at once.

Very unusual and fun!

CORN PUDDING

2 C. fresh corn, cut from cob
2 tsp. sugar
1 1/2 tsp. salt
1/4 tsp. black pepper
3 eggs, slightly beaten
2 T. butter
2 C. milk

In a large bowl, combine corn, sugar, salt and pepper. Add eggs; mix well. In a saucepan, add butter to milk and heat just until butter melts. Stir into corn mixture. Pour into buttered 1-quart casserole dish. Bake in preheated 350° oven for 1 hour. Makes 6 servings.

EGGPLANT CASSEROLE

1 lg. eggplant
1 onion, grated
1 rib celery, cut up
1 C. Cheddar cheese, grated
2 eggs, beaten
1/2 C. bread crumbs or
    crushed corn flakes
5 strips bacon, fried
Salt and pepper, to taste

Dice eggplant and cook in boiling, salted water until done. Fry bacon and crumble; saute onion in same pan. Cool and drain eggplant. Mash until smooth. Add eggs, 2/3 of cheese and remaining ingredients. Reserve 1/3 of cheese. Cook for 30 to 40 minutes at 350°. Put reserved cheese on top and return to oven for a few minutes until cheese is melted. Serves 6 to 8.

FRIED EGGPLANT

1 med. eggplant, peeled
1 tsp. salt
1 egg, beaten
Cornmeal
Cooking oil

Cut eggplant into 1/2" strips. Cover with water mixed with 1 teaspoon salt. Soak for 1/2 hour; drain. Dip in beaten egg; roll in cornmeal and deep fry. Makes 6 servings.

SOUTHERN FRIED OKRA

1 lb. fresh okra, washed and drained
3/4 C. self-rising flour
1 tsp. salt
1 egg
1/2 C. milk
1 C. yellow cornmeal
Oil, for frying

Remove stems and ends of each pod of okra. Cut into 3/4 to 1" slices crossways. In one bowl, mix flour and 1/2 teaspoon salt; in another, beat egg, 1/4 teaspoon salt and milk until frothy. In another bowl, place cornmeal. Heat oil in skillet 1 1/2 to 2" deep. Dip okra slices first in the flour mixture to coat; then in the egg mixture and lastly in the cornmeal. Place okra into hot oil a few pieces at a time. Cook 5 minutes, stirring to brown evenly. Drain on paper towels. Serves 4.

BAKED VIDALIA ONIONS

4 med. Vidalia onions
1/2 stick butter
Salt and pepper, to taste
4 bouillon cubes

Peel and cut onions in half. Lay cut side up in a baking dish. With a knife, cut a small hole in each and place 1/2 bouillon cube and pat of butter in each. Salt and pepper to taste. Cover with foil and bake at 350° for 40 to 45 minutes. Serve hot. Serves 4 to 6.

Note: If you can't find Vidalia onions, use any variety you like.

GLAZED ONIONS

16 sm. white onions, peeled
1/4 tsp. salt
1/2 tsp. sugar
1/2 C. water
2 T. butter
Ground black pepper or paprika

Place onions, salt, sugar and water in a saucepan that has a tight-fitting lid. Boil gently for about 10 minutes (add more water if necessary, but only a little). Reduce heat to low. When onions are tender and all liquid has disappeared, add butter and saute onions. Garnish with ground black pepper or paprika.

SWEET ONION BAKE

7 1/2 C. sweet onions, chopped
4 T. butter
1/2 C. raw rice
5 C. boiling, salted water
3/4 C. grated Swiss cheese
2/3 C. Half and Half

Saute onions in butter. Cook rice in water for 5 minutes. Drain and mix with onions; add cheese and cream. Bake uncovered at 300° for 1 hour.

Beatrice McCurry Miller
(One of the Twelve)
Charleston, SC

VIDALIA ONION PIE

1 C. dry bread crumbs
1/4 C. butter, melted
2 C. Vidalia onions, sliced thin,
    or yellow skin onions
2 T. butter (for saute)
3 eggs
3/4 C. Half and Half
3/4 tsp. salt
1/4 tsp. pepper
3/4 C. grated sharp Cheddar cheese
Paprika
Parsley, chopped, to garnish

Combine bread crumbs and melted butter. Press into an 8 or 9" pie plate (glass). In a skillet, saute onions in 2 tablespoons butter just until transparent. Spoon onions into crust. Beat together eggs, Half and Half, salt and pepper. Pour over onions. Layer cheese over top, then sprinkle with paprika. Bake at 350° for 30 to 35 minutes. Garnish with parsley.

Very good with Wheat Thins. Just dip them and enjoy.

GINGERED GEORGIA PEACHES

2 16-oz. cans sliced peaches in heavy
   syrup, drained (reserve juice)*
1 tsp. ground ginger
10 whole cloves
1 or 2 cinnamon sticks**

*Six large fresh peaches may be substituted (peel, pit and slice).

**May substitute 1 teaspoon lemon zest.

Drain peaches and reserve juice; set aside. In a saucepan, combine juice, ginger, cloves and cinnamon sticks; bring to a rolling boil. Reduce heat to simmer and cook 10 to 12 minutes. Add drained peaches to hot mixture. Simmer until peaches are heated through. Makes 6 to 8 servings.

Serve hot or cold with poultry and pork.

SOUTHERN BLACK-EYED PEAS (USING DRIED PEAS)

1 16-oz. bag dried black-eyed peas
1 ham hock or 1/4 lb. fatback
2 tsp. salt
1 tsp. Tabasco sauce (or more)
1 lg. onion, peeled (stem end intact)
1 pkg. Sweet 'N Low (or other
   powdered sugar substitute)
Water
Baking soda

Pick over peas and remove undesirable broken ones or bits of trash. Pour boiling water over peas in a bowl; add pinch of baking soda. Soak for 1 or 2 hours. Drain. In a large pot, place soaked peas, salt, Tabasco sauce, onion and sugar substitute with enough water to fill 2" above peas. Cover and boil gently over medium heat until peas are just tender. If you boil them too long or too fast, you'll have mush! Add just enough water to keep barely covered. Serves 6 to 8.

Peas more than double in volume when cooked. Dried peas and beans are very good for you and most economical.

BETH'S ENGLISH PEA CASSEROLE

1 16-oz. can English peas, drained
1 can mushroom soup
1 C. grated cheese
1 stack Ritz crackers, crushed
1/2 stick butter, melted

Place peas and soup in casserole dish. Mix well. Top with cheese and cracker crumbs. Pour melted butter over top. Bake uncovered at 325° for 20 minutes, until bubbly.

Beth Radford Ashmore
Lincolnton, GA

PINEAPPLE/CHEESE SOUFFLE

1/2 stick butter or margarine
1 C. granulated sugar
4 eggs, beaten
1 15-oz. can crushed pineapple,
    drained
5 slices white bread, crusts
    trimmed and cubed
3/4 C. grated sharp Cheddar cheese

Cream butter and sugar; fold in eggs and mix well (use an electric hand mixer or whisk). Add pineapple and bread cubes. Stir. Pour into a buttered 9x9" casserole dish. Sprinkle with cheese. Bake at 350° for 40 to 50 minutes. Serves 4 to 6.

Very good with ham or any pork dish. Serve hot.

AUNT "B'S" POTATOES

5 or 6 potatoes, peel and
    slice in 1/4" rounds
1 onion, chopped
Oregano, paprika, salt and pepper,
    and garlic salt, to taste
1 stick margarine

Melt margarine in large skillet. Add all ingredients on medium heat. Cook approximately 20 minutes. Stir every now and then until done.

Good.

Betty Miller Wilkins
Prosperity, SC

GOLDEN SPUDS

4 med.-sized baking potatoes
3 T. melted butter or margarine
1/3 C. finely crushed corn flakes
1/2 tsp. salt
1/2 tsp. basil
Mayonnaise

Boil potatoes (unpeeled) for 20 to 30 minutes or until almost done. Peel. Mix corn flakes, salt and basil. Coat each potato with mayonnaise and roll in corn flake mixture until coated. Place on a buttered baking sheet. Bake uncovered at 500° for 30 minutes. Makes 4 servings.

HOT POTATO SALAD

4 lg. potatoes, diced or
    cut in 1/2" rounds
5 slices bacon
1/2 C. finely chopped onions
1 1/2 T. flour
1 tsp. powdered dry mustard
1 1/2 tsp. salt
1 T. sugar
3/4 C. water
1 egg, beaten
1/3 C. vinegar

Boil potatoes until tender in salted water. Drain. Cook bacon in a skillet until crisp. Remove bacon and chop in small pieces. Use 2 tablespoons bacon drippings to cook onion until golden brown. Remove from heat, add flour, mustard, salt and sugar. Stir well. Stir in water. Boil 2 minutes. Beat the egg in a small bowl. Add 2 tablespoons hot mixture; stir well. Add this back to hot mixture. Add vinegar and reheat. Pour hot mixture over potatoes; top with bacon. Serve hot.

LEMON POTATOES

1 1/2 lb. small new potatoes, well
    scrubbed (approx. 1 doz.)
1/4 C. olive oil
2 T. lemon juice
1 tsp. grated lemon peel
1/4 tsp. freshly ground black pepper
1 T. minced parsley or chives

Place potatoes in a pot of salted water. Cover and cook for 15 to 16 minutes over medium heat. While potatoes are cooking, mix olive oil, lemon juice, peel and pepper. Set aside. Drain potatoes. Keep in pot and cook a little more until potatoes are dry. Shake pot several times during this time. Pour potatoes into a shallow, heated serving dish. Prick each one several times with tines of a fork. Pour olive oil mixture over potatoes and stir to coat. Sprinkle with parsley or chives and serve hot. Makes 4 to 6 servings.

MASHED POTATO CASSEROLE

2 C. cooked, mashed white potatoes
1 C. grated Cheddar cheese
3 eggs, beaten well
1/2 tsp. salt
1/8 tsp. pepper
1/2 tsp. chopped chives (optional)
1 T. butter

Mix ingredients well. Bake immediately at 350° for 45 minutes. Serve hot.
Note: Sprinkle additional grated cheese on top if you wish before baking.

POTATO CHEESE BALLS

1/2 C. grated American cheese
1/2 tsp. seasoned salt
2 C. mashed potatoes
1/2 C. bread crumbs
1 egg, beaten
1 tsp. chopped chives (optional)
1 T. milk

In a mixing bowl, combine cheese, salt and potatoes. Shape into 6 balls. Roll in bread crumbs. In a separate bowl, blend egg and milk. Dip potato balls in this mixture. Place on a baking sheet. Bake at 450° for 15 minutes. Makes 6 servings.

ROASTED RED POTATOES WITH ROSEMARY

12 med.-size red potatoes
1/4 C. olive oil
6 cloves garlic, minced
1 tsp. dried rosemary, crumbled
Salt and pepper, to taste

In a large pot, boil potatoes in salted water just until tender (approximately 20 minutes). Drain and cool. Peel potatoes (if you wish) and cut in half. Place in large baking sheet (with sides). Combine oil, garlic and rosemary. Pour over potatoes and stir to coat on all sides. Add salt and pepper to taste. Bake in preheated 375° oven for 1 hour, until crisp and lightly browned. Turn several times while baking. Serve hot.
Good with beef or pork.

SKINNY FRIES

4 lg. baking potatoes
1 T. Cajun seasoning spice
1 or 2 egg whites (do not beat)
Vegetable oil spray (Pam)

Cut potatoes in strips as for French fries or in rounds. Do not peel. Sprinkle with Cajun spice. Put egg whites in a large bowl. Place potato strips or rounds into whites and toss to coat. Add more Cajun spice if you like. Coat a large cookie sheet with vegetable spray. Place a single layer of potatoes on sheet and spray top with vegetable spray. Bake at 400°. Stir and turn to brown on all sides.

These are great and low in fat.

STUFFED POTATOES

8 baking potatoes
1/2 C. butter or margarine (soft)
1 8-oz. ctn. sour cream
1 1/2 C. shredded Cheddar cheese
Salt and pepper, to taste

Bake potatoes at 425° for 60 minutes or until done. Allow to cool to touch. Slice 1/3 of skin from one side of each potato. Carefully scoop out potatoes; leaving shells intact. Combine potatoes, butter, salt and pepper, sour cream and 1 cup cheese. Whip until smooth. Stuff shells with mixture. Bake at 350° for 25 minutes. Remove from the oven and sprinkle remaining 1/2 cup cheese on tops and return to oven for 5 minutes. Serves 8.

A great do ahead dish that can be refrigerated several hours or overnight. A beautiful sight on a buffet table and delicious with ham. Men even ask for this recipe!

GRATED SWEET POTATO PUDDING

3 C. raw sweet potatoes,
  peeled and grated
2 C. water
1 1/2 C. granulated sugar
2 eggs, slightly beaten
1/2 stick butter or margarine, melted
1 tsp. grated orange rind
1 tsp. ground nutmeg
1/4 tsp. ground cloves
1/4 tsp. allspice
1/2 tsp. cinnamon
1 tsp. vanilla
1 C. toasted coconut (optional),
  topping

Combine pudding ingredients in order listed. Pour into buttered 9x13" baking dish. Bake at 325° for 2 hours. Stir at least 3 times during baking. During last 5 minutes, top with toasted coconut if you wish. Let stand 10 minutes before serving. Serves 6 to 8.

Note: This is as close to Nannie's as possible.

PEACHES AND SWEET POTATOES

1 16-oz. can sliced peaches
1 29-oz. can sweet potatoes, drained
1/2 C. brown sugar (packed)
3 T. butter or margarine
1/2 tsp. cinnamon
1/2 tsp. nutmeg

Drain the peaches and set juice aside. Place peaches and sweet potatoes in a buttered 9x13" casserole dish. Stir together lightly. In a saucepan, combine juice from peaches, brown sugar and butter. Bring to a boil. Reduce heat to simmer and cook 5 minutes more. Stir gently once or twice. Remove from heat and pour mixture over peaches and potatoes. Sprinkle cinnamon and nutmeg on top. Bake uncovered at 325° for 30 minutes.

Enjoy!

TERESA'S SWEET POTATO SOUFFLE

3 C. cooked, mashed sweet potatoes
1 C. granulated sugar
1 stick margarine
1 T. vanilla
3 eggs, beaten
1/2 tsp. salt

Combine ingredients. Pour into buttered 9x13" casserole dish. Sprinkle Topping over and bake for 30 minutes at 350°. Serves 8 to 10.

Topping
1 stick margarine
1 C. chopped nuts
1 C. brown sugar
1/2 C. self-rising flour

Cut margarine into 16 pieces and mix with remaining ingredients. Sprinkle on top of potato mixture.

Teresa McCurry Tankersley
Lincolnton, GA

SPINACH CASSEROLE

3 10-oz. pkg. frozen, chopped spinach,
    cooked and drained
2 3-oz. pkg. cream cheese
1 T. grated lemon rind
Salt and pepper, to taste
Dash nutmeg
1 sm. pkg. Pepperidge Farm dressing
    mix, crushed into crumbs
1/2 stick margarine, melted

Cook spinach as per directions on package. Drain. Add cream cheese while hot. Add lemon rind, salt, pepper, 1/4 cup margarine and nutmeg. Mix gently. Top with crushed dressing mix which has been mixed with remaining melted butter. Bake at 350° for 25 minutes. Serves 8 to 10.

Serve hot.

FRIED SQUASH

4 med.-size squash, thinly sliced
3 eggs, beaten
1/2 C. milk
1 tsp. salt
2 C. cornmeal or 2 C. self-rising flour
Oil, for frying

Wash squash in cold water. Drain. Leave peelings on. Slice thinly; set aside. Heat oil in skillet. Combine beaten eggs, milk and salt to make batter. Dip slices in batter and fry until done. Serves 6.

PLANTATION SQUASH CAKES

3 C. boiled squash, mashed when cold
1 egg
1 tsp. baking powder
1 C. sugar
Pinch salt

Mix the ingredients and add enough flour to make batter a little thicker than required for batter cakes. Fry like batter cakes; sprinkle with sugar and serve with meat dish for luncheon or dinner.

Note: You may use eggplant instead of squash.

SIMPLE SQUASH CASSEROLE

2 C. cooked yellow squash, mashed
1 sm. onion, chopped
1 C. shredded sharp Cheddar cheese
1 sm. can evaporated milk
3 eggs
Salt and pepper
2 T. butter or margarine

Boil squash and onion until just slightly tender (parboiled). Beat eggs and milk together. Mash cooked squash and onion with a fork until lumpy. Salt and pepper to taste. Fold squash mixture into egg mixture. Fold in cheese. Pour into baking dish. Dot with butter. Bake at 350° for 30 minutes. Serve hot. Makes 6 servings.

Reheats well in microwave

SQUASH CASSEROLE II

4 C. cooked yellow squash, drained
1 onion, chopped
1 T. sugar
1 egg
1/2 C. mayonnaise
1/2 C. sour cream
1 C. sharp cheese, grated
1/2 C. pecans, chopped fine
1/2 stick butter
Salt and pepper, to taste
Pecan halves (optional)
Bread or cracker crumbs or
    grated cheese

Add butter to squash and mash. Mix onion, sugar, egg, mayonnaise, sour cream, cheese, pecans, salt and pepper; add to squash. Pour mixture into casserole dish. Top with crumbs or grated cheese. Dot with butter. Decorate with pecan halves if desired. Bake at 350° for 35 or 40 minutes or until brown. Yield: 8 to 10 servings.

Ruby McCurry Matthews
(One of the Twelve)
Lincolnton, GA

SQUASH CASSEROLE III

3 C. cooked yellow squash, drained
2 eggs, beaten
1/2 tsp. black pepper
1 tsp. salt
1 C. milk
1 1/2 C. herb stuffing mix (dry)
1 C. chopped onion
3/4 stick margarine or butter
1 C. grated sharp Cheddar cheese

Reserve 1/2 cup dressing and 1/2 cup grated cheese. Mix other ingredients in a large bowl. Pour into a buttered 2-quart casserole dish. Top with remaining dressing and cheese. Bake at 375° for 40 to 45 minutes. Cool 5 minutes before serving. Serves 6.

Leftovers reheat nicely in microwave.

SQUASH CASSEROLE IV

2 1/2 lb. yellow squash
1 lg. onion, chopped
1/2 stick butter
1 can cream of mushroom soup
1/2 pt. sour cream
2 eggs, beaten
2 T. butter or margarine
Salt and pepper, to taste
1 sm. bag Pepperidge Farm
    dressing mix
1 stick butter or margarine, melted

Saute onion in 1/2 stick butter. Boil squash in salted water; drain and mash. Add chopped sauteed onion, soup, beaten eggs and sour cream. Mix well. Salt and pepper to taste. Mix dressing with stick of melted butter. Put 1/2 dressing in squash mixture and stir gently. Top with remaining dressing. Bake at 325° for 30 to 45 minutes. Makes 6 to 8 servings.

FRIED GREEN TOMATOES

3 med. green tomatoes
1 1/2 C. self-rising flour
1 tsp. salt
1/2 tsp. pepper
1 C. buttermilk
Oil, for frying (Crisco)

Wash tomatoes, remove stems and slice 1/4" thick. Set aside. Heat oil in heavy skillet on medium/high heat. In a shallow bowl, mix flour with salt and pepper. Place buttermilk in a small bowl. Dip one slice at a time into buttermilk; then into flour mixture, coating well. Fry in deep, hot oil. Do not let burn. Watch carefully. Drain on paper towels. Serve immediately. Add salt to taste. Makes 6 to 8 servings.

Good with fried chicken or fish.

Note: This procedure may be used to fry any green or yellow vegetable.

BAKED STUFFED TOMATOES

6 firm ripe tomatoes
1 can niblet corn, drained
1 T. finely chopped onion
1 T. finely chopped green pepper
1/2 tsp. dried basil
1/4 tsp. pepper
1/2 tsp. salt
1 1/2 T. melted butter
6 to 8 T. buttered bread crumbs

Wash the tomatoes, wipe dry and cut a slice from the stem end; scoop out the seeds and pulp (do not break skin of tomato). Set aside. Mix pulp, corn, onion, green pepper, salt and pepper, basil and melted butter together. Stir to blend and fill each tomato equally. Top with buttered bread crumbs. Bake at 325° for 30 to 40 minutes, until tomatoes are soft and crumbs are brown. Remove carefully to a serving plate with a wide spatula. Makes 6 servings.

SPINACH STUFFED TOMATOES

6 lg. tomatoes

Slice piece off top of tomatoes and scoop out centers. Place on paper towels upside down to drain. Set aside.

Stuffing:
1 16-oz. pkg. frozen, chopped spinach, thawed and drained well
1 C. whole milk
3 T. flour
3 T. butter or margarine
1/2 C. grated cheese
1/2 tsp. seasoned salt

Place all ingredients in a saucepan and cook on medium heat stirring until thick. Remove from heat. Set aside.

Sprinkle a little salt and pepper inside each tomato and fill each with hot mixture. Top with the following mixed in a small bowl: 1/2 cup bread crumbs and 1/4 cup grated cheese. Bake at 350° for 15 to 25 minutes. Makes 6 servings.

TURNIP GREENS WITH CORN DODGERS

1 ham hock
2 qt. water
2 tsp. salt
2 lg. bunches turnip greens
1/2 C. sugar
1 T. Tabasco sauce
1 T. white wine

Wash turnip greens leaf by leaf (both sides) under running cold water. Trim tough stems with scissors. Place 2 quarts water in large pot; add salt and ham hock. Boil covered for 20 minutes. Place washed and trimmed greens in boiling water a few at a time. Pour sugar over top. Add Tabasco and wine. Cook covered over medium heat until greens are tender. Cook Corn Dodgers in pot liquor. Serve hot. Makes 6 to 8 servings.

Note: Turnip greens will cook down. Add water if needed just to cover during cooking.

Corn Dodgers:
2 C. plain cornmeal
2 T. bacon drippings
1 sm. onion, minced
Salt and pepper
Turnip green pot liquor (boiling hot)

In a bowl, mix cornmeal, drippings and onions with enough pot liquor to hold dough together (dough should be stiff but moist). Add salt and pepper to taste. Roll a tablespoon at a time between palms of hands and flatten with fingers. Place in very hot pot liquor from greens. Boil gently on low until fairly firm. Serve in a bowl with broth from pot.

MIXED VEGETABLE CASSEROLE

1 16-oz. pkg. mixed vegetables,
   cooked according to package
   directions or 2 cans Veg-All
   mixed vegetables, drained
1 C. chopped celery
1 C. chopped onions
1 C. grated Cheddar cheese
1 C. mayonnaise

Mix all ingredients and place in buttered 9x13" casserole dish. Sprinkle with Topping and bake uncovered at 325° for 20 to 25 minutes, until brown.

Topping:
1 C. crushed saltines
1 stick butter, melted

Sprinkle saltines over casserole. Then drizzle butter over top.

- SAUCES & TOPPINGS -

BECHAMEL SAUCE

2 T. butter or margarine
2 T. plain flour
1 T. minced onion
1 C. chicken broth
2 T. heavy cream
Salt and pepper, to taste

In a saucepan, melt butter, stir in flour with a fork or wire whisk. Stir rapidly until smooth. Stir in onion, then broth. Stir constantly until thickened. Add cream in a thin stream, stirring all the while. Add salt and pepper. Simmer on very low heat for 12 to 15 minutes. Makes approximately 1 cup.

Good on vegetables.

CHEESE SAUCE

1 2/3 C. evaporated milk
1/2 tsp. salt
2 C. grated American cheese

In a saucepan, mix milk and salt. Cook for 2 minutes over medium heat. Add cheese; stir until smooth. Makes approximately 2 cups.

Good over vegetables and seafood.

GREEN ONION BUTTER

1 stick butter
2 1/2 tsp. onion powder
1 1/2 tsp. chopped parsley

Melt 4 tablespoons butter in a saucepan. Add onion powder and parsley. Stir constantly over low heat until mixture is golden. Cool for 10 minutes; cream in remaining 4 tablespoons butter. Shape or mold as desired. Chill 1 hour and serve over meats or vegetables. Makes 6 servings.

Great with baked potatoes!

VEGETABLE CASSEROLE TOPPING

1/2 C. butter, melted
1/2 C. bread crumbs
1/2 C. finely chopped nuts

Combine the melted butter, bread crumbs and nuts in a small bowl. Mix well.

Great topping for broccoli, English peas, squash, asparagus or spinach casseroles.

Poultry
&
Seafood

- CHICKEN -

BAKED BREADED CHICKEN

1 chicken, cut into pieces or
   6 chicken breast halves
1/2 tsp. Tabasco sauce
2 T. olive or vegetable oil
1 T. butter, melted

Wash chicken pieces in cold water; pat dry. Put Tabasco sauce, oil and melted butter in a 9x13" casserole dish. Roll each piece of chicken in the butter mixture, then place 1 piece at a time, in a paper bag or Ziploc bag containing Breading. Shake well and return breaded chicken pieces to the casserole dish containing the butter mixture. Bake at 350° for 35 to 40 minutes or until chicken is done.

Breading:
1/3 C. cornmeal
1/3 C. bread crumbs
3 T. flour
1 tsp. salt
Dash cayenne pepper

Combine ingredients.

BAKED CHICKEN SALAD

4 C. cooked chicken, diced
3/4 C. mayonnaise
3/4 C. cream of chicken soup
1 tsp. salt
2 C. chopped celery
4 eggs, cooked and sliced
1 tsp. finely minced onion
2 T. lemon juice

Mix together and place in large baking dish. Mix together Topping and sprinkle over chicken mixture. Chill several hours or overnight. Bake at 400° for 30 minutes. Serves 8.

Topping:
1 C. crushed potato chips
2/3 C. shredded Cheddar cheese
1/3 C. chopped almonds

Combine ingredients.

ELEGANT CHICKEN SALAD

3 C. cooked chicken, cubed or
   6 boneless, skinless chicken
   breasts, boiled in salted water
1 sm. can diced pineapple, drained
1/4 C. shredded coconut
1/2 tsp. curry powder
1/2 C. sour cream
1/2 C. chopped walnuts
1 tsp. lemon juice
1/2 C. mayonnaise
1/2 C. diced celery
1/2 tsp. celery seeds
1 apple, diced
Paprika, to garnish

Boil chicken in water seasoned with 1/2 teaspoon salt. Remove chicken from water and cube into 1" pieces. Place chicken in large mixing bowl. Add remaining ingredients to chicken and mix well. Chill and serve on lettuce leaves and garnish with a sprinkle of paprika. Serves 6 to 8.

BUTTERMILK BAKED CHICKEN

1 whole chicken, cut in pieces,
   washed and patted dry
1 1/2 C. buttermilk
1 1/2 C. all-purpose flour
Salt and pepper, to taste
Water, enough to cover chicken
1/2 tsp. paprika (optional)

Twelve to twenty-four hours prior to cooking, place the cut up chicken in a bowl with the buttermilk. Cover tightly; store in refrigerator. When ready to cook, remove the chicken (one piece at a time) from the buttermilk and dip each piece in flour. Place chicken pieces in a 13x9" casserole dish. Sprinkle evenly with salt, pepper and paprika. Cover with water and bake uncovered at 350° for 45 minutes. Makes 4 to 6 servings.

CASHEW CHICKEN CASSEROLE

1 can Chinese noodles (reserve
   3/4 C. for topping)
1 can cream of mushroom soup
1/4 C. water
2 6-oz. cans white meat chicken
1/4 lb. whole salted cashew nuts
1 C. finely diced celery
1/4 C. finely chopped green onion

Mix part of Chinese noodles (reserve 3/4 cup) with remaining ingredients. Mix well and place in buttered 9x9" casserole dish. Top with reserved noodles. Bake at 325° for 40 minutes. Serve hot. Makes 4 servings.

Note: White Albacore tuna may be substituted.

CHARLESTON CHICKEN

8 chicken breasts, skinned and boned
8 thin slices bacon
1 4-oz. pkg. dried beef, chopped
1 10-oz. can mushroom soup
1 C. dairy sour cream

Wrap chicken breasts with bacon and place in casserole dish. Sprinkle dried beef over top. Combine soup and sour cream, then spoon over chicken. Bake uncovered for 3 hours at 275°. Makes 8 servings.

Serve with brown rice (see Table of Contents).

CHICKEN A LA ORANGE

1 broiler-fryer chicken, cut or quartered
Juice from 1 lime
1 tsp. salt
1/2 tsp. pepper
3/4 tsp. paprika
Oil
1/2 C. lemon juice
1 C. orange juice

Marinate chicken in lime juice for 1 hour. Remove from juice; season with salt, pepper and paprika. Brown in oil. Place in baking dish. Pour combined juices over top. Bake at 375° for 45 minutes or until tender. Makes 4 servings.

CHICKEN & DRESSING CASSEROLE

6 chicken breast halves or 3 lb. fryer
1 C. chopped celery
1 sm. onion, chopped
Salt and pepper, to taste
1 pan cornbread (bake while
   chicken is cooking)
1 can cream of chicken soup
1 can cream of celery soup
2 C. chicken broth
1/4 tsp. sage or poultry seasoning

Boil chicken, celery, onion and seasonings in enough water to more than cover chicken until chicken is tender. Debone chicken. Cut into finger size pieces. Crumble cornbread into a buttered 13x9" casserole dish. Add soups, broth, chicken and seasonings. Mix very well. Add more broth if too dry. Bake at 350° for 30 to 35 minutes. Serves 8 to 10.

Serves best if allowed to cool a few minutes.

CHICKEN & DUMPLINGS I, II, III

Boil a 3-pound chicken in water with celery and onion. Add salt and pepper to taste. Reserve broth. Remove chicken from broth and cool enough to debone. Return to broth.

Egg Dumplings I:
1 1/2 C. all-purpose flour
3 T. shortening
1/2 tsp. salt
1 egg, beaten
Water

Mix all ingredients with enough water to make a soft dough. Roll out on a floured surface and cut in 2" strips or 2" squares. Let dry for 30 minutes. Drop in boiling broth with chicken. Cover and cook for 12 minutes. Do not uncover during cooking time (this applies to I, II and III).

Plain Dumplings II:
2 C. flour
1/2 C. soft butter
1/3 C. milk or enough to hold together

Combine ingredients, roll and cut into strips, and drop into boiling broth. Cook covered for 12 to 15 minutes until done.

Dumplings III:
3 cans refrigerated biscuit dough
   (plain, not the flaky kind)

Open can and cut each biscuit in fourths. Drop into boiling broth. Cook covered for 12 minutes until done.

CHICKEN CASSEROLE

2 10-oz. pkg. frozen broccoli
2 C. cooked chicken
1 C. mayonnaise
1 can cream of chicken soup
1 can cream of mushroom soup
1/2 tsp. curry powder
1 tsp. lemon juice

Cook and drain broccoli. Spread broccoli, then layer chicken. Mix next 5 ingredients and pour on. Sprinkle with Topping and dot top of casserole with margarine. Bake at 350° for 30 minutes.

Topping:
1/2 C. bread crumbs
1/2 C. shredded Cheddar cheese
1 T. margarine, dotted on top

Combine bread crumbs and cheese.

Betty Miller Wilkins
Prosperity, SC

CHICKEN DIVAN

6 boneless, skinless chicken breast
   halves, boiled in water
   with 1/2 tsp. salt
2 10-oz. pkg. frozen broccoli spears,
   cooked and drained
2 cans cream of chicken soup
1 C. mayonnaise
1 tsp. curry powder
1 C. sharp cheese, grated coarsely
1 C. bread crumbs or
   1 C. dry Pepperidge Farm
   herb seasoned dressing
1 T. melted butter or margarine

Cut cooked chicken in pieces (about the size of your little finger). Place broccoli in a buttered baking dish; place chicken pieces atop broccoli. Mix soup, mayonnaise, curry powder and cheese; pour over chicken. Mix melted butter with bread crumbs or dressing and sprinkle on casserole. Bake at 350° for 25 minutes. Makes 6 to 8 servings.
Divine!

QUICK CHICKEN DIVAN

2 (6 1/2-oz.) cans boneless
   white chicken, drained
2 10-oz. pkg. frozen, chopped broccoli,
   cooked according to package
   directions and drained well
1 C. grated sharp Cheddar cheese
1 can cream of mushroom soup or
   1 can cream of chicken soup
1/2 C. milk

In a 9x13" glass baking dish, layer chicken, broccoli and cheese. Mix the milk and your choice of soup together in a small bowl and pour over other ingredients. Cover baking dish with foil. Bake at 350° for 10 minutes, covered. Remove foil and bake for 10 minutes more. Makes 4 servings.

CHICKEN MAGNOLIA

Poaching Liquid:
1 rib celery, cut in 3 pieces
1 carrot, cut in 3 pieces
1 sm. onion, cut in 3 pieces
1 bay leaf
1 qt. water

5 to 6 lb. boneless, skinless chicken
    breasts, cut in bite-size pieces

Sauce:
7 T. plain flour
1 tsp. dry mustard
1/8 tsp. Accent
1/2 tsp. sugar
1 tsp. salt
1/4 tsp. nutmeg
1/8 tsp. cayenne pepper
1/2 tsp. paprika
3 T. butter
2 C. Poaching Liquid
2 C. Half and Half cream
1 8-oz. can sliced water chestnuts
1/4 C. cream sherry or Madeira
1 lb. fresh sliced mushrooms

Combine ingredients for Poaching Liquid in a large pot. Cook for 15 to 20 minutes, covered. Remove vegetables and bay leaf. Add chicken pieces and bring back to boil. Reduce heat to medium and cook for 5 to 8 minutes, covered. Remove chicken to a heated platter. Cover with foil.

In a small bowl, combine flour and spices. In a large pot, melt butter; add flour mixture and stir until smooth. Slowly add broth and cream. Stir until smooth. Add chestnuts, sherry and chicken. Add sliced mushrooms. Cook on low, stirring, for 5 minutes. Serve over Party Rice (see Table of Contents). Serves 16 to 20.

Flo Pursley
Lincolnton, GA

CHICKEN POT PIE

1 chicken, boiled and boned
1 can Veg-All, drained
1 can English peas, drained
2 cans cream of chicken or
    mushroom soup
1 C. all-purpose flour
3/4 C. milk
1 stick melted butter

Place chicken in bottom of 9x13" dish with 2 cups of chicken broth. Layer vegetables and soup., Mix flour, milk and butter. Pour over vegetables and chicken. Bake at 350° for 1 hour or until brown.

Lynda Rogers
Manchester, GA

MELT-IN-YOUR MOUTH CHICKEN PIE

1 3-lb. fryer
2 C. reserved chicken broth
1 can cream of chicken soup
1 C. self-rising flour
1 tsp. salt
1/2 tsp. pepper
1 C. buttermilk
1 stick margarine, melted

Cook chicken until tender. Remove meat from bones and skin. Reserve broth. Cut chicken into small pieces and place in 9x13" pan. In a saucepan, bring to a boil the broth and soup. In another bowl, combine flour, salt, pepper, buttermilk and margarine. Mix thoroughly to form batter. Pour broth mixture over chicken. Spoon batter over top. Bake at 425° for 25 to 30 minutes.

CHICKEN SKILLET DINNER

1 1/2 lb. chicken breasts,
  boneless, skinless
1 1/2 tsp. salt
1/4 tsp. pepper
2 T. butter or margarine
1 C. thinly sliced green onions
  with tops
1 8-oz. can sliced mushrooms,
  drained (keep liquid)
1/2 C. cooking sherry
1 pkg. frozen English peas
1 1/2 C. chicken broth
2 tomatoes, peeled and cut in eighths
1 tsp. basil
2 T. cornstarch
Liquid from can of mushrooms

Cut chicken in strips; season with salt and pepper. Saute in butter until browned. Fold in onions and mushrooms; cook for 3 minutes on medium heat. Add sherry, peas and chicken broth. Cover; let simmer for 25 minutes. Add tomatoes and basil. Dissolve cornstarch in liquid from mushrooms. Add to chicken mixture. Cook about 5 to 6 minutes more. Serve over rice or noodles. Serves 6.

COMPANY CASSEROLE

2 sm. chickens, boiled and deboned
  (reserve 3/4 C. chicken broth)
4 C. cooked rice
1 can cream of chicken soup
1 can cream of celery soup
1/2 C. butter or margarine
1 C. sherry
1/2 tsp. pepper
1 tsp. salt
1/2 tsp. celery salt
2 C. Pepperidge Farm
  herbed dressing mix

After deboning cooked chicken and cooking rice, combine all ingredients except dressing mix and chicken broth in a large mixing bowl. Stir well. Pour into a buttered 9x13" glass casserole dish. Mix chicken broth and 2 cups dressing mix. Spread on top of casserole. Bake at 350° for 25 to 30 minutes until bubbly and dressing is browned. Serves 8.

CREAMED CHICKEN

2 C. diced, cooked chicken
3 T. butter
1 T. chopped celery
1 T. chopped onion
1/4 C. plain flour
1 C. chicken broth (from cooking
  chicken or canned)
1 C. milk
3/4 tsp. salt
1/4 tsp. pepper
1 tsp. chopped parsley

In a heavy skillet, saute celery and onion in butter until tender (but not browned). Add flour. Stir, using a fork or wire whisk, until well blended. Stir in the chicken, broth and milk and cook until it forms a smooth sauce, stirring all the while. Add chicken, seasonings and parsley. Serve on toast points or on split shortcake. Makes 4 servings.

Note: To vary this recipe, use only 1 1/2 cups chicken and then add 1/2 cup sauteed mushrooms or 1/2 cup English peas.

FANCY CHICKEN

12 chicken breasts, boned
1 loaf bread, crust removed and
    made into fine bread crumbs
    (dried overnight)
3/4 C. grated Parmesan cheese
1/4 C. chopped parsley
1 clove garlic, minced
2 tsp. salt
1/4 tsp. pepper
2 sticks butter, melted

Topping:
1/3 C. Parmesan cheese
1/4 C. butter
1 T. plus 1 tsp. sherry
1 can cream of chicken soup
Bread crumbs
Melted butter

Mix bread crumbs with cheese, parsley and seasonings. Dip each piece of chicken in melted butter, then in crumb mixture. Place chicken in shallow baking dish. Do not allow pieces to touch. Drizzle with 2 tablespoons of butter. Place chicken on top and cover with Topping. Bake at 350° for 1 hour.

Sprinkle Parmesan cheese and 1 tablespoon sherry over chicken. Dot with 1/4 cup butter. Pour cream of chicken soup on top with 1 teaspoon sherry. Top with bread crumbs and drizzle with butter.

Good for a family or company dinner.

GOLDEN BAKED CHICKEN

1 chicken, cut into serving pieces
2 T. margarine
1 T. paprika
1/2 tsp. dried oregano
1/2 C. flour

Mix flour, paprika and oregano in a paper bag or Ziploc plastic bag. Add 1 piece of chicken at a time and shake bag to coat chicken. Melt margarine in a 9x13" glass baking dish. Place coated chicken in baking dish and cover with foil. Bake at 375° for 1 hour. Remove foil for last 20 minutes of cooking time, making sure that chicken is turned once to brown on each side. Makes 4 servings.

HERBED CHICKEN

2 T. all-purpose flour
1/4 tsp. sage
1/4 tsp. dried thyme
1/4 tsp. dried basil
4 skinless, boneless
    chicken breast halves
2 T. margarine or butter
1 can cream of chicken soup
1/2 C. water

Combine flour, sage, thyme and basil in a bowl. Coat chicken lightly with this mixture. Place margarine or butter in a skillet over medium-high heat. Brown chicken for 10 minutes on each side. Push chicken to one side of skillet; stir in soup and water. Reduce heat to low. Cover and simmer for 15 to 20 minutes. Makes 4 servings.

LEMON CHICKEN

6 boneless, skinless
  chicken breast halves

Marinade:
5 T. lemon juice
3 T. Dijon mustard
2 cloves garlic, finely chopped
1/4 tsp. white pepper
5 T. olive oil

Sauce:
2 C. chicken broth
1 tsp. cornstarch (dissolved
  in 1 T. water)
2 T. orange marmalade
2 T. butter
2 T. fresh chopped parsley
1/2 tsp. red pepper flakes
1 C. sliced almonds
Thin lemon slices, for garnish

Combine Marinade ingredients. Add chicken breasts to Marinade in large Ziploc bag. Marinate 1 hour. Turn several times. Remove chicken from Marinade. Reserve Marinade. Saute chicken breasts in a skillet in 1 tablespoon olive oil until browned on both sides. Remove from skillet.

Saute almonds in 1/2 tablespoon oil; set aside. Pour the following into skillet: Strained Marinade, chicken broth and cornstarch mixture. Cook over medium-high heat until Sauce reduces to half, 4 or 5 minutes. Add marmalade and stir in butter, parsley and pepper flakes. Return chicken to skillet and bake at 350° for 30 to 40 minutes. Add almonds and garnish with lemon slices. Serve. Makes 6 servings.

NANA'S CHICKEN SQUARES

1 3-oz. pkg. cream cheese
3 T. butter
2 C. cooked chicken, diced
1/4 tsp. salt
1/8 tsp. pepper
2 T. milk
1 T. chopped chives
1 8-oz. can crescent rolls
3/4 C. seasoned bread crumbs

Blend soft cheese and 2 tablespoons butter until smooth. Add next 5 ingredients. Mix well; separate dough in 4 rectangles and seal seams. Spoon 1/2 cup on center of dough, close and seal. Brush top with rest of butter. Sprinkle top with butter and bread crumbs. Bake at 350° for 20 to 25 minutes.

Beatrice McCurry Miller
(One of the Twelve)
Charleston, SC

PICATTA FOR CHICKEN, VEAL OR PORK TENDERLOIN

4 T. flour
1/2 stick butter

Sauce:
Juice of 1 lemon
1/4 C. white wine
Salt and pepper, to taste
1/2 lemon, sliced
Parsley or cilantro sprigs

Place boneless chicken breast or veal or medallions of pork tenderloin between plastic wrap and pound until very thin. Dust with flour and saute in butter (3 minutes on each side). Add Sauce ingredients. Simmer for 3 to 5 minutes more. Serve garnished with lemon slices and parsley or cilantro sprigs.

PINEAPPLE CHICKEN

1/2 lb. boned chicken breasts, diced
1/4 C. green pepper, cut in thin strips
1 T. red sweet pepper, cut in thin strips
   (optional)
4 T. oil
1/2 C. pineapple chunks, drained
   (juice reserved)
2 T. chicken broth
1 T. vinegar
3 T. pineapple juice (from
   can of pineapple)
2 T. sugar
1/2 C. plum sauce or grape jam

In a wok or heavy skillet, heat oil until hot. Stir-fry chicken and pepper strips. When chicken turns white, add remaining ingredients and stir-fry 4 to 5 minutes on medium-high heat. Makes 4 servings.

Colorful and tasty!

Note: Chicken broth can be frozen in ice trays. One "cube" equals 1 tablespoon. A great convenience when only a little broth is needed.

PRESERVED CHICKEN

6 chicken breast halves
1 12-oz. jar peach preserves*
1 env. onion soup mix (dry)
1 8-oz. bot. Russian dressing

Place chicken breasts in baking dish, skin side down. Mix peach preserves, onion soup mix and Russian dressing together and spread 1/2 of the mixture on chicken. Bake at 325° for 25 minutes. Turn chicken over; pour rest of sauce over chicken and bake for 55 to 60 minutes more. Serve hot over white rice. Makes 6 servings.

*Apricot preserves may be substituted.

RITZY CHICKEN

6 to 8 chicken breasts
2 cans cream of chicken soup
1 8-oz. ctn. sour cream
1 stack Ritz crackers, crumbled fine
2 tsp. poppy seeds
1 1/2 sticks butter or margarine,
   melted

Bake chicken covered for 1 hour. Cut cooled chicken into bite-size pieces. Place in 9x13" casserole dish. Mix soup and sour cream and pour over chicken. Crumble Ritz crackers; add poppy seeds and sprinkle on top of other ingredients. Drizzle melted butter over top. Bake at 350° for 25 minutes. Makes 6 to 8 servings.

A good company or Sunday lunch dish.

SAUTEED CHICKEN STRIPS

**4 boneless, skinless chicken breasts,
cut in finger-size strips across**
3 T. butter or margarine
3 T. olive oil
1/2 tsp. salt
1/4 tsp. garlic pepper
1/2 tsp. thyme
1 T. chopped parsley
1/2 C. wine (red or white)

Place olive oil and butter or margarine in heavy skillet over medium-high heat. Add chicken strips; sprinkle with salt, garlic pepper, thyme and parsley. Saute 5 to 7 minutes, stirring all the while. During the last minute, add wine and stir. Makes 4 main-dish servings or 24 to 30 appetizer servings.

Very quick to prepare. Good with Honey Dijon dressing.

SOUTHERN FRIED CHICKEN (2 WAYS)

2 1/2 to 3 lb. cut up chicken

Wash chicken in cold water; pat dry.

I Seasoned Flour:
1 1/2 C. all-purpose flour
1 T. garlic salt
1 1/2 tsp. black pepper
1 1/2 tsp. paprika
1/4 tsp. poultry seasoning

In a large Tupperware bowl with a lid, place all ingredients. Put the lid on and shake well. Add a few pieces of chicken at a time to the flour mixture, replacing the lid and shaking well to coat chicken. Fry in hot Crisco shortening or oil (about 3" deep), turning once or twice, until golden brown, about 10 minutes per side on medium-high heat.

II Crispy Batter:
2/3 C. all-purpose flour
1/2 tsp. salt
1/8 tsp. pepper
1 beaten egg yolk
3/4 C. flat beer or water

Combine ingredients in a bowl. Dip each piece of chicken in the batter and fry in hot oil, 10 minutes on each side or until done, turning once or twice.

Cover the frying pan with a lid while cooking. Watch carefully.

VELVET CHICKEN

3 eggs
3 T. milk
1/2 tsp. salt
4 boneless, skinless chicken breasts
1/2 C. grated Parmesan cheese
1/2 C. butter, melted in skillet
1 C. cooking sherry

Beat eggs and milk together. Add salt to chicken. Dip chicken in egg/milk mixture; roll in cheese. Melt butter in electric skillet on medium heat (300°). Add coated chicken and brown on both sides. Add sherry; cover. Reduce heat to 225°. Cook for 45 minutes. Makes 4 servings.

Serve over noodles or wild rice.

- TURKEY -

TURKEY ASPARAGUS CASSEROLE

1 can chicken or turkey broth
1 can Cheddar cheese soup
1 1/3 C. Minute rice
1 can cut asparagus, drained
2 C. turkey, cut in thumb-size pieces*
1 T. melted butter or margarine
Paprika

Reserve 1/2 cup soup. Place remaining half of soup and broth in a heavy skillet over medium heat. When mixture comes to a boil, remove from heat and stir in rice. Place drained asparagus and turkey pieces over top. Stir remaining soup with 1 tablespoon melted butter and pour evenly over turkey. Cover and simmer for 5 minutes. Garnish with paprika. Makes 6 servings.

Great for leftover turkey!

Note: Chicken or ham may be substituted.

TURKEY FILLED PATTY SHELLS

Filling:
2 C. cooked turkey, cut in 1" cubes
1/3 C. beef consomme
1 1/2 C. very thinly sliced celery
1 C. coarsely chopped, salted, roasted almonds
1 C. Hellmann's mayonnaise
2 T. grated onion
2 T. lemon juice
1 sm. can English peas/carrots, drained
1/4 tsp. freshly ground pepper
Dash paprika

6 baked patty shells
1/2 C. grated sharp Cheddar cheese

In a saucepan, combine turkey and consomme. Cook over medium heat until turkey is heated (approximately 4 minutes). Reduce heat and add remaining Filling ingredients. Cook over low heat for 6 minutes.

Fill patty shells with hot mixture. Top with cheese and bake at 350° for 5 minutes. Serve right away. Makes 6 servings.

Great for leftover turkey.

Note: Chicken may be substituted.

UNCLE PIERCE'S CAJUN FRIED TURKEY

1 fresh turkey breast or whole turkey
    (8 to 10 lb.)
1 6-oz. bot. Tabasco sauce

Wash thoroughly. Put in clean plastic bag with Tabasco sauce. Seal. Put in refrigerator for 24 hours, turning several times. Heat enough oil to 350° to cover bird in fish cooker. Cook 3½ minutes per pound, turning frequently to keep from burning on bottom.

For those who "like it hot", with a large gauge meat injector (can be bought at some grocery stores - called "Cajun Injector"), inject Tabasco into turkey in 6 to 8 areas.

Pierce McCurry
(One of the Twelve)
Alpharetta, GA

GRAVY FOR CHICKEN PIE

1 stick butter
1/4 C. plain flour
3 C. chicken broth
2 egg yolks
1/2 C. Half and Half

Using your favorite chicken pie ingredients, add this creamy gravy in place of soups if you wish.

Melt butter over medium heat in a saucepan. Add flour; stir and cook until slightly boiling. Add chicken broth (from cooking your chicken for pie or canned broth). Cook until smooth and thickened somewhat. Add egg yolks and cream. Pour immediately over pie ingredients and top with crust.

MARMALADE MAYONNAISE SAUCE

3/4 C. mayonnaise (Hellmann's
    reduced calorie)
1 T. orange marmalade
1/2 tsp. ground ginger
1/4 tsp. chopped fresh mint (optional)

Combine ingredients in a bowl.
Good on turkey sandwiches.

PEACH CATSUP

1 #2 can Cling peach slices
   in heavy syrup
1 med. onion, minced
1/2 C. vinegar
1/2 tsp. cinnamon
1/4 tsp. ground cloves
1/4 tsp. allspice
1/4 tsp. salt
Few grains of cayenne pepper

Place syrup from peaches in a saucepan and boil until reduced to 1/2 cup. Add remaining ingredients. Boil gently until onion and peaches are soft and mixture has thickened (takes about 1 hour). Cool and put through a sieve. Chill. Serve with poultry or pork. Makes about 1 1/2 cups.

SEASONED FLOUR (FOR FRYING CHICKEN)

2 C. self-rising flour
1/4 C. powdered milk
1 1/2 T. paprika
Salt and pepper, to taste

Combine ingredients. This is enough "flour" for 3 cut up chickens.

UNCLE HAMMOND'S BARBECUE SAUCE

1 gal. Twelve Oaks distilled vinegar
1 C. sugar
3 T. black pepper
1 C. Worcestershire sauce
2 T. red hot pepper (cayenne)
3 T. salt
2 sticks butter
4 32-oz. bot. catsup

Combine ingredients. Bring to a rolling boil. Reduce heat and cook for 1 hour.

For barbecued chicken. Omit catsup and Worcestershire sauce for pork.

*Aunt Joann's husband and a grand cook. This recipe was a secret for over 30 years.

*Hammond Ferguson**
Lincolnton, GA

- FISH -

FRIED CATFISH BITES

Crisco, for frying
2 eggs, beaten
1 C. milk
Salt and pepper, to taste
2 lb. catfish fillets, cut
   in bite-size pieces

Put Crisco in deep iron skillet over medium-high heat. Mix eggs and milk. Salt and pepper the catfish pieces. Dip first into egg/milk mixture. Roll in corn-meal and fry. Turn once; drain on paper towels. Serve hot with hushpuppies. Makes 6 to 8 servings.

BAKED STUFFED FISH

3 to 4 lb. fish (bass or trout)
2 T. butter
2 T. chopped scallions
2 T. finely chopped green pepper
1 med. tomato, coarsely chopped
1 T. chopped parsley
Salt and pepper
1/2 C. dry bread crumbs
   (cornbread dressing mix)
1 thinly sliced onion
1 thinly sliced green pepper
Sprigs of fresh dill
4 T. melted butter
1/2 C. dry vermouth
1 T. lemon juice
Salt and pepper

Remove backbone from fish. Combine 2 tablespoons butter, scallions, 2 tablespoons green pepper, tomato, parsley, salt, pepper and bread crumbs. Stuff fish. Tie with string. Brush bottom of baking dish with butter. Place fish in center of dish. Surround with onion, 1 green pepper and fresh dill. Pour 4 tablespoons butter, vermouth, lemon juice, salt and pepper over fish. Bake at 400° for about 30 minutes to 1 hour, basting often. Makes 4 servings.

Beatrice McCurry Miller
(One of the Twelve)
Charleston, SC

BROILED FISH FILLETS

1 lb. fish fillets (any kind)
1 stick butter, melted
1/4 C. dry vermouth or dry white wine
3 T. grated Parmesan cheese
3 T. bread crumbs

In a saucepan, melt butter; add vermouth or wine and pour over fish in a shallow baking pan. Broil until liquid is brown, approximately 8 to 10 minutes. In a small bowl, mix cheese with bread crumbs. Sprinkle over fillets. Broil until brown. Makes 2 to 3 servings.

Fast and delicious!

FRIED FISH

2 or 3 lb. fish, cleaned and
   cut into serving pieces
1 C. shortening
2 T. salt
1/2 C. cornmeal

Heat shortening in heavy skillet over medium heat. Mix salt and cornmeal; roll fish pieces in mixture. Fry in skillet until lightly browned.

PEPPERED OCEAN PERCH

1 pkg. frozen ocean perch (fillets),
   unbreaded
Salt, to taste
Lemon pepper, to taste
Paprika, to taste
Red pepper flakes, to taste
Butter, to taste

Place frozen or thawed fillets in glass baking dish. Sprinkle seasonings over both sides of fillet. Top with butter. Bake with skin side down at 325° for 30 minutes, until flaky.

DILLED SALMON SHORTCAKES

Shortcakes:
2 1/2 C. Bisquick
3 T. butter or margarine
1/2 C. milk
1/2 tsp. dillweed

Preheat oven to 450°. Mix Bisquick, butter, milk and dillweed to form a soft dough. Knead several times on floured surface. Roll about 1/2" thick. Cut in equal size rounds. Bake on a buttered cookie sheet.

Sauce:
1 10-oz. can cream of mushroom soup
3/4 C. milk
2 tsp. lemon juice
1 15-oz. can salmon, skin and
   bones removed
1/4 tsp. Tabasco sauce

While Shortcakes are baking, combine all ingredients in a saucepan and bring to a boil. Split Shortcakes in half. Pour hot Sauce mixture over bottom half and cover with top half. Makes 6 servings.

SALMON CASSEROLE

1 1-lb. can salmon, drained
1 egg, beaten
3 T. butter, melted
1 can cream of mushroom soup
1 C. bread crumbs
Salt and pepper, to taste

Mash salmon; mix with soup; add beaten egg and seasonings. Place in baking dish. Top with bread crumbs. Drizzle with butter. Bake uncovered at 325° for 30 minutes.

SALMON CROQUETTES AND SAUCE

1 1-lb. can salmon, drained
1/2 C. flour
1 C. cornmeal
1 tsp. soda
2 tsp. grated onion
2 eggs, beaten
1 C. buttermilk

Place salmon in large bowl; stir and mash with fork until flaky. Add remaining ingredients. Shape into balls (a little larger than a golf ball, but not as large as a tennis ball). Drop balls carefully into hot oil and fry until brown; drain on paper towels and serve while hot.

Sauce may be omitted as these are great with maple syrup!

Sauce:
3 T. butter
3 T. flour
3/4 tsp. salt
1 1/2 C. milk
1 T. lemon juice
1 1/2 T. parsley flakes
Dash paprika

Melt butter in pan over medium heat. Add flour; stir until consistency of paste. Add salt. Gradually add milk; stir until thick. Let bubble gently for about 2 minutes, stirring all the while with a wire whisk. Remove from heat; stir in lemon juice, parsley and paprika. Serve at once.

SALMON PATTIES (FRIED)

1 16-oz. can salmon, drained
1/2 C. flour
1 C. cornmeal
1 tsp. soda
2 eggs, beaten
1 C. buttermilk
Oil, for frying

Remove skin and bones; mash with a fork in a mixing bowl; add flour, cornmeal, soda, eggs and buttermilk. Shape into small patties (silver dollar size). Heat oil in heavy skillet. Drop patties carefully into hot oil and fry until brown. Drain on paper towels. Serve hot. Makes 8 to 10 servings.

These are so good with syrup!

SALMON SUPPER

1 C. water
2 C. frozen green peas
2 carrots, coarsely grated
1 tsp. instant minced onion
1/4 tsp. dried thyme
1/4 tsp. dried dill
1 can cream of mushroom soup
1 C. milk
2 1/4 C. Minute rice
1 15-oz. can pink salmon, drained,
    skin and bones removed
2 C. crushed potato chips

In a skillet with a lid, place water, peas, carrots, onion, thyme, dill, soup and milk. Bring mixture to a boil. Add rice and salmon; reduce heat to simmer, cover and cook for 5 to 7 minutes. Remove from heat and top with crushed potato chips. Let stand 5 minutes. Serve right from skillet. Makes 4 to 6 servings.

Supper in less than 15 minutes. Only 1 cooking utensil to wash!

CREAMED TUNA IN BREAD CUPS

1 loaf French bread, unsliced
Butter, melted
2 7-oz. cans white tuna, drained
2 cans cream of chicken soup
1 sm. can LeSueur English peas,
    drained
2 tsp. chopped pimiento
Salt and pepper, to taste

Cut bread into 8 slices, 2 1/2" thick. Trim off crusts. Hollow center out with a sharp knife. Butter bread and removed centers generously and toast until golden brown in moderate 350° oven. In a saucepan, combine drained tuna, soup, drained peas, pimiento and salt and pepper to taste. Heat until bubbling. Fill toasted bread cups with hot mixture. Top with toasted center. Makes 8 servings.

Note: Canned white chicken may be substituted for tuna.

- SHELLFISH -

CAROLINA CRAB CAKES

2 T. melted butter
2 T. minced onion
1 tsp. dry mustard
3/4 tsp. salt
1/4 tsp. pepper
1 T. mayonnaise
1 egg, well beaten
1 lb. regular crab meat
1/2 C. dry bread crumbs
Optional seasonings*

*For more highly seasoned cake, add pepper sauce, Worcestershire sauce and horseradish.

Saute onion in butter; combine seasoning, mayonnaise, beaten egg and crab meat. Shape into 8 patties and refrigerate for several hours. When ready to fry, coat crab cakes with bread crumbs. Preheat griddle. Brown cakes on lightly buttered griddle for 2 to 4 minutes per side.

Enjoy!

Betty Miller Wilkins
Prosperity, SC

SOUTHERN CRAB CAKES

2 C. fresh crab meat or
   2 cans crab meat
Salt and pepper, to taste
2 T. flour
1 C. seasoned bread crumbs
2 eggs, beaten
1/2 C. chopped green onions
2 tsp. dillweed
2 tsp. Italian seasoning
1/4 tsp. cayenne pepper
2 sticks butter or margarine

In a mixing bowl, combine crab meat, salt, pepper, flour, bread crumbs, eggs, onions, dillweed, Italian seasoning and cayenne. Mix well. Shape into 4" cakes and fry in hot butter until lightly brown on both sides. Makes 8 servings.

CRAB OR SHRIMP MOUSSE

6 oz. cream cheese, room temperature
1 C. mayonnaise
1 C. celery, chopped fine
1 sm. onion, grated
1 T. unflavored gelatin
1 can cream of mushroom soup
6 oz. frozen or fresh shrimp or crab

Dissolve gelatin in 1 tablespoon hot water and add to warmed soup. Beat with cream cheese and mayonnaise. Add other ingredients and salt to taste. Pour into mold sprayed with Pam. Refrigerate. Unmold and serve with crackers.

Betty Miller Wilkins
Prosperity, SC

BROILED LOBSTER

1 to 1 1/2 lb. live lobster, claws
  removed and split in half
1/2 C. olive oil
Salt and paprika, to taste

Crack the claws. Place claws and lobster halves in a small baking pan. Cover with olive oil, sprinkle with salt and paprika. Broil 15 minutes. Serve with wedges of lemon and hot, melted butter. Makes 2 servings.

Note: Have someone in the seafood department remove the claws and split the lobster for you!

FRIED OYSTERS

1 pt. fresh oysters, drained
1 1/2 to 2 C. all-purpose flour
1/2 tsp. salt
1/8 tsp. pepper
1 beaten egg
1/2 C. milk
3 C. cracker meal
Shortening, for frying (about 2" deep)

Drain oysters; set aside on paper towels. In one bowl, mix flour, salt and pepper. In another bowl, mix egg and milk until well blended. In another bowl, place cracker meal. Dip each drained oyster first in flour mixture, then in egg and milk mixture; then in cracker meal. Place oysters on a cookie sheet in a single layer after coating and chill for 1 hour. Have shortening very hot and about 2" deep. Fry 6 to 8 oysters at a time in a single layer. Makes 4 servings.

PEPPERED OYSTERS

4 doz. oysters, poached in
  oyster liquid and drained
2 T. olive oil
1 T. lime juice
2 T. black peppercorns
6 sm. cloves garlic, peeled
Salt, to taste
1 or 2 bay leaves

Poach oysters in oyster liquid for 4 to 5 minutes. Drain. Place olive oil in a large skillet. Heat oil and add oysters. Add lime juice. Add remaining ingredients. Turn oysters once and simmer for 5 minutes.

AUNT SYLVIA'S GOLDEN FRIED SHRIMP

1/4 C. all-purpose flour
1/4 C. cornstarch
1/8 tsp. salt
1/4 C. beer or white wine
1 egg yolk
2 T. melted butter or margarine
1 lb. lg. shrimp, peeled
Puritan oil, for frying

Combine flour, cornstarch and salt in a small bowl. Add beer, egg yolk, and butter; beat until smooth. Dip shrimp in butter and fry in hot oil.

Sylvia Herring McCurry
Wife of Don McCurry
(One of the Twelve)
Thomson, GA

BOILED SHRIMP

1 T. salt
4 lb. med. or lg. fresh shrimp
2 gal. water
2 T. Old Bay seafood boil
   (or your favorite spices)
2 lemons, quartered
Additional seasoning, for garnish

First wash shrimp in cold water. Then cover with water and salt. Let stand for 5 to 10 minutes. Drain. Bring 2 gallons water, seasonings and lemon wedges to a rolling boil. Add shrimp and stir. Cook for 2 to 3 minutes or until shrimp are pink. Drain in large colander. Serve on a large shallow platter and garnish with a small amount of additional seasoning. Cool or chill. Peel and eat. Serves 6 to 8.

BOOM BOOM'S PICKLED SHRIMP

3 lb. jumbo shrimp,
   shelled and deveined
3 C. white vinegar
12 whole allspice
9 whole cloves
3 bay leaves
2 T. sugar
1 T. salt
3/4 tsp. crushed black pepper
1 red onion, peeled and sliced
2 T. snipped fresh dill or
   2 tsp. dried dillweed

Bring 6 cups water to boiling in large saucepan. Add shrimp, and return to boiling. Reduce heat, and simmer, uncovered, 6 minutes. Drain, and set aside. In same saucepan, combine 1/3 cup water with the vinegar, spices, bay leaves, sugar, salt, and pepper; bring to boiling. Reduce heat, and simmer, uncovered, 5 minutes. In large bowl, layer shrimp with onion and dill. Add hot vinegar mixture. Let stand until cold; then refrigerate, covered, at least 24 hours before serving. Makes 10 to 12 servings.

Betty Miller Wilkins
Prosperity, SC

CURRIED SHRIMP

1 lb. med. raw shrimp
1/4 C. butter
1/3 C. chopped onion
1/4 C. chopped green pepper
1 clove garlic, minced or mashed
1 tsp. curry powder
3 T. flour
Boiling, salted water
2 C. Half and Half
1 tsp. lemon juice
1/2 tsp. salt
1/8 tsp. ground ginger
1/8 tsp. pepper
1/8 tsp. chili powder
Hot, cooked rice

Cook shrimp in boiling, salted water until they turn pink, about 5 minutes. Drain and cool, then shell, devein and set aside. In a pan or chafing dish, over direct heat, melt the butter; add onion and green pepper and saute until tender, about 5 minutes. Add garlic, curry powder and flour; heat and stir until bubbly. Remove from heat and stir in the cream, lemon juice, salt and remaining seasonings. Cook, stirring, until thickened. Add the shrimp and heat through. Taste, and add more curry or salt, if needed. Set over hot water to keep warm (it keeps well up to 2 hours). Serve over hot, cooked rice. Makes about 4 to 5 servings.

Betty Miller Wilkins
Prosperity, SC

GULF SHRIMP

12 lg. shrimp (uncooked),
    peeled, tails left on
1/2 C. teriyaki sauce
6 strips bacon

Place peeled shrimp in a Ziploc bag or shallow glass dish. Pour teriyaki sauce over shrimp. Chill for 1/2 hour. Partially cook bacon. Cut each slice in half. Remove shrimp from teriyaki sauce. Wrap each shrimp with 1/2 strip of bacon, secured with a toothpick. Broil until bacon is crisp, turning to brown evenly. Remove toothpicks and serve. Increase ingredients to make more servings. Makes 4 servings.

LOW COUNTRY BOIL

3 T. commercially prepared shrimp boil
    (Old Bay seasoning) plus 3 T. salt
    or 3 T. homemade boil
1 1/2 gal. water
2 lb. hot, smoked link sausage, cut
    into 2" pieces (Hillshire Farm)
12 ears freshly shucked corn,
    broken into 3 to 4" pieces
4 lb. shrimp (raw)

In a large stockpot, add the seasoning to the water and bring to a boil. Add the sausage and boil, uncovered, for 5 minutes. Add the corn and count 5 minutes. Add the shrimp and count 3 minutes. (Don't wait for the liquid to return to a boil before timing the corn and shrimp.) Drain immediately and serve.

Note: This is beautiful served in a large shallow platter or huge wooden or glass bowl.

MARINATED SHRIMP

1 lb. lg. shrimp, washed, peeled and
    deveined (leave tails on)
1/2 C. sherry
1/2 C. soy sauce
1/2 C. peanut oil
1 clove minced garlic
1/2 T. ground ginger or
    1 T. minced fresh ginger
1/2 tsp. celery seed

Place shrimp in glass bowl or 1 gallon Ziploc plastic bag. Combine remaining ingredients. Pour over shrimp and marinate for 3 to 6 hours. Remove from marinade. Charbroil on grill or broil in oven for 3 to 4 minutes on each side. Baste with marinade. Makes 4 servings.

SHRIMP CAROLINE

6 C. boiled shrimp, cook in salted
    water (1 tsp. salt to 1 qt. water)
2 C. soft bread crumbs (may use 6
    slices bread, cut in small cubes)
2 sticks butter (do not use margarine)
2 garlic cloves, minced finely
1/3 C. chopped fresh parsley or
    1 T. dried parsley
1/2 tsp. paprika
1/4 tsp. mace
1/4 tsp. Tabasco sauce or dash of
    cayenne pepper
2/3 C. cooking sherry

Cook shrimp in boiling water. Drain, peel and remove tails. Set aside. Make bread crumbs. Set aside. Place butter, garlic cloves, parsley, paprika, mace and Tabasco or pepper and sherry in a large bowl. Add bread crumbs and toss to coat.

Place shrimp in buttered 9x13" glass casserole dish. Pour sauce and bread crumbs over shrimp and bake in preheated 325° oven for 20 to 25 minutes. Serves 6 to 8.

SHRIMP SCAMPI

2 lb. raw shrimp (med. or lg.)
1/2 C. olive oil
2 cloves garlic, minced fine
2 tsp. salt
1/3 C. chopped parsley
    (reserve 1/2 for garnish)
1 lemon, sliced in wedges

Peel and devein shrimp. Place shrimp in a single layer in a buttered, shallow baking dish or in individual ramekins. Pour a thin stream of the olive oil over shrimp. Sprinkle shrimp with garlic, salt and 1/2 of parsley. Place oven rack approximately 4 1/2" from heat. Broil 5 to 7 minutes on each side, according to size of shrimp. When done, sprinkle with remaining parsley. Garnish with lemon wedges.

SHRIMP SHORTCAKE

2 1/2 C. Bisquick or other
   packaged biscuit mix
3 T. melted butter or margarine
1/2 C. milk
1 7-oz. can med. shrimp or
   1/2 lb. cooked, fresh shrimp,
   chopped coarsely
1 10-oz. can cream of shrimp soup
1/2 C. milk
2 tsp. lemon juice
1/4 C. chopped chives

For Shortcake: Preheat oven to 450°. Make a soft dough from Bisquick, butter and milk. Knead a few times on a floured piece of foil or board. Roll out 1/2" thick. Cut into 6 equal rounds. Bake on buttered cookie sheet for 10 to 12 minutes.

While shortcake is baking, combine remaining ingredients; bring to a boil; reduce heat to simmer. Remove shortcake from oven. Split and place one on each serving plate. Pour shrimp mixture over bottom half of shortcake. Cover with top half. Serves 6.

SKILLET SEAFOOD CASSEROLE

1/2 stick butter or margarine
1/2 tsp. MSG
Salt and pepper, to taste
3/4 lb. peeled shrimp
3/4 lb. crab meat
1/2 C. shredded, sharp
   Cheddar cheese
2 T. sherry
1/4 tsp. ground mace
Few grains cayenne pepper (optional)

In an electric skillet, saute crab meat and shrimp until barely browned; add salt, pepper, sherry and mace. Spread mixture to cover bottom of skillet. Top with cheese; cover and simmer until cheese is melted. Serve from the skillet. Serves 6 to 8.

Wonderful!

BEER BATTER

1 C. flour
2 T. cooking oil
1 1/2 tsp. salt
1 C. beer
2 egg whites, beaten until frothy

Mix first 4 ingredients, then fold in egg whites. Use as a batter for seafood, mushrooms or onion rings or just about anything you want to deep-fry.

Easy!

SAUCE FOR FISH

1 C. Hellmann's mayonnaise
1 T. parsley flakes
1 T. tarragon leaves
1 T. grated onion
1 T. lemon juice
1/4 tsp. grated lemon peel (optional)

Combine all ingredients; mix very well. Refrigerate until serving.

May be used with any kind of fish, cooked any way.

Beef & Pork

- BEEF -

AUNT JOANN'S MEAT SAUCE

1/2 lb. pork sausage
1 lb. hamburger meat
1 med. onion, chopped (optional)
1 #2 can tomatoes
2 tsp. chili powder

Put sausage, hamburger meat and onion in a frying pan with a little butter. Let cook until meat is white; then add tomatoes and chili powder. Cook on low heat until meat is done. Add a little water if it's too thick. Serve over cooked spaghetti noodles.

Note: Add a little more chili powder and a can of kidney beans and this doubles as chili!

Recipe is 45 years old.

Joann McCurry Ferguson
(One of the Twelve)
Lincolnton, GA

BEEF BEAN SKILLET

1 lb. ground chuck
2 C. barbecued baked beans
    (or kidney)
1/2 C. chopped onion
1/2 C. diced celery
2 T. bacon drippings
1 1/2 C. canned tomatoes, drained
    (#303 can)
1/4 C. catsup
1 1/2 tsp. Worcestershire sauce
Dash Tabasco sauce
1 tsp. salt
Pinch of pepper
1/4 tsp. dried oregano
1/4 C. dry red wine
1 T. bottled steak sauce

Heat bacon drippings and saute onion and celery. Add beef and brown. Add remaining ingredients, cover and simmer 15 to 20 minutes until flavors are well blended. Makes 4 to 6 servings.

BURGER BAKED BEANS

1/2 lb. ground beef
1 can pork and beans
1 can pinto beans
1 med. onion, chopped
1/2 tsp. garlic powder
1/2 C. brown sugar
1 T. mustard
1 T. maple syrup
1 T. Worcestershire sauce
1/2 C. catsup
3 slices uncooked bacon, cut in
    9 equal pieces (for topping)

Brown ground beef until crumbly. Drain. In a 9x13" casserole dish, combine pork and beans, chopped onion, garlic powder, brown sugar, mustard, syrup, Worcestershire sauce and ketchup. Stir. Place bacon pieces on top. Bake at 250° for 3 hours. Makes 8 servings.

Good with hot dogs! Great with barbecue, too!

CHUCK ROAST

3 to 4 lb. chuck roast
2 T. olive oil or vegetable oil
1 lg. onion, sliced in rings
3/4 C. sliced celery
3/4 C. sliced carrots
1 tsp. minced garlic
1 C. dry red wine
1 tsp. salt
1/2 tsp. pepper
1/2 tsp. dried thyme
2 bay leaves

Place oil in a large ovenproof pot (a deep iron skillet is perfect) over medium heat. When oil is hot, add roast and sear on all sides. Add remaining ingredients. Stir. Bake in same pot as directed. Cover tightly with foil or lid. Bake at 325° for 2½ to 3 hours. Remove bay leaves when roast is done. Remove roast; let stand for 10 to 15 minutes loosely covered. Slice across grain and serve with sauce. Makes 8 servings.

Note: To thicken sauce of vegetables, etc., add 3 tablespoons flour mixed with 1 cup water to pot and cook on surface unit until thickened.

EASY CHEESY CASSEROLE

1 1/2 lb. ground beef
1/2 med. onion, chopped
Salt and pepper, to taste
1/4 tsp. garlic salt
1 can Cheddar cheese soup
1 can tomato sauce
1/2 bx. shell macaroni,
    cooked and drained
1 C. shredded Cheddar cheese

Brown beef and onions in a skillet. Drain. Place in 9x13" casserole dish. Stir in cooked and drained macaroni, cheese soup, and tomato sauce. Mix well. Season to taste with salt, pepper and garlic salt. Top with shredded cheese. Bake at 350° for 30 minutes. Makes 6 to 8 servings.

Serve hot with a green salad and French bread.

ELEGANT STEAK AND RICE

1 1/2 lb. tenderized boneless
    beef round steak
1 1/2 T. vegetable oil
2 lg. onions, cut in 1/2" slices
    and separated into rings
1 4-oz. can sliced mushrooms,
    drain (reserve liquid)
1 (10 3/4-oz.) can condensed
    cream of mushroom soup
1/2 C. dry sherry
1 1/2 tsp. garlic salt
3 C. hot, cooked rice

Cut steak into thin strips. In a large skillet (oven-proof, if desired), brown meat in oil, using high heat. Add onions and mushrooms. Saute until tender-crisp. Blend soup, sherry, liquid from mushrooms, and garlic salt. Pour over steak. Heat and serve over rice.

"FOILED AGAIN" (OVEN DINNER)

Aluminum foil
1 1/2 lb. ground round
8 med. potatoes, peeled and quartered
8 carrots, cut into lengthwise strips
2 onions, sliced
2 ribs celery, cut in 2" strips
4 pats butter
Salt and pepper, to taste
Parsley flakes, to taste
Garlic salt, to taste
Butter

Make ground round in fairly thick patties about 7" in length and 5" wide. Place on large sheet of foil, top with potatoes, onions, carrots, celery, butter pats, spices and butter. Fold foil up and seal around ingredients. Place in a large baking dish. Bake at 350° for 45 minutes. Do not open until finished. Remove carefully to serving plate.

Smells and tastes yummy!

FRANKFURTER CASSEROLE

2 1-lb. pkg. beef frankfurters
2 cans "chili-hot" beans or
    pork and beans
1/2 C. catsup
1/2 tsp. garlic salt
1/4 C. granulated sugar
1 T. prepared mustard
1 T. minced onion
Sharp Cheddar cheese
Bacon slices

In a large casserole dish, combine beans, catsup, garlic salt, sugar, mustard and onion. Split each frankfurter lengthwise (not quite all the way through bottom). Cut a piece of cheese to fit opening in each frank and place atop beans in casserole dish. Cut bacon into 3" lengths and place atop franks. Bake at 350° for 35 to 40 minutes or until bacon is browned and cheese is melted. (Don't overcook or cheese will melt away.) Serves 8 to 10.

GEORGIA CORN DOGS

3/4 C. self-rising flour
1/4 C. self-rising cornmeal
1 T. granulated sugar
1 tsp. dry mustard
2 T. grated onion
1 egg, beaten
1/2 C. milk
1 lb. beef hot dog franks
Peanut oil, for cooking

In a large bowl, combine flour, corn-meal, sugar, mustard and onion. Set aside. Combine egg and milk in separate bowl. Pour into flour mixture. Roll franks in mixture; fry in 2 1/2" deep peanut oil until golden brown. Makes 6 servings.

GRILLED IN BUTTER FRANKS

1 1-lb. pkg. beef frankfurters
1/2 stick butter or margarine
Buns

Melt butter in a heavy skillet. Add frankfurters. Cook over medium-low heat "rolling" frankfurters in butter until lightly browned, about 8 to 10 minutes. Place each frankfurter in a bun and top as desired. Makes 10 servings.

GRILLED SEASONED BURGERS

2 lb. lean ground beef
4 T. chopped chives
3 T. A-1 steak sauce
1/2 tsp. steak salt
1/4 tsp. black pepper
6 hamburger buns with sesame seeds
    or 6 onion rolls
Mayonnaise, Dijon mustard, to taste
6 leaves lettuce
6 slices tomato
6 slices onions in rings

Start fire in outdoor grill. In a large bowl, mix ground beef, chives, steak sauce, steak salt and black pepper. Shape mixture into 6 equal patties about 3/4" thick. Rub grill rack with oil and place 4" over hot coals. Grill burgers on both sides until desired doneness is achieved. Spread heated rolls or buns with choice of condiments, top with lettuce, tomato and onion rings. Makes 6 servings.
Note: May broil in oven indoors.

HAMBURGER PIE

1 9" pie shell, partially cooked
1/2 lb. lean ground beef
1/3 C. chopped green onion
1/2 C. mayonnaise
1/2 C. milk
2 eggs, beaten
Salt and pepper
1 T. cornstarch
1/2 lb. sharp Cheddar cheese, grated
    (reserve half for topping)

Brown ground beef and onion in a skillet. Drain. Blend mayonnaise, milk, eggs and cornstarch until smooth. Stir in ground beef and half of cheese. Pour into partially baked pie shell and top with remaining cheese. Bake at 350° for 35 to 45 minutes. Serves 6 to 8.
Slice in wedges. Serve hot.

HASH BROWNED BEEF

1 6-oz. bx. Idaho hash browns
   (any brand will do)
2 1/2 C. boiling water
2 T. melted butter or margarine
1 1/2 lb. ground beef
   (made into 6 patties)
Steak salt, to taste
1 med. onion, sliced into rings
1 (14 1/2-oz.) can tomatoes,
   chopped in liquid
1 tsp. basil
1 tsp. salt
1 tsp. pepper

In a 9x13" buttered casserole dish, place hash browns, water and butter. Top with ground beef patties, steak salt and onion rings. In a separate bowl, mix tomatoes, basil, salt and pepper and pour over patties and potatoes. Bake, uncovered, at 400° for 45 minutes. Makes 6 servings.

LAYERED SKILLET DINNER

6 slices bacon, cut in 1" pieces
1 lb. ground beef, made into 4 patties
1/2 tsp. salt
1/4 tsp. pepper
2 onions, peeled, sliced into rings
4 to 6 potatoes, peeled and sliced
   about 1/3" thick
4 to 6 carrots, sliced about 1/3" thick
1/4 C. chopped green pepper
1 T. chopped parsley
1/4 C. water

In a deep skillet, place bacon pieces, then top with 4 ground beef patties; sprinkle with a little salt and pepper. Then layer the onions, potatoes, and carrots. Sprinkle each layer with the salt and pepper. Top with green pepper and parsley. Cook on medium heat about 3 minutes after bacon begins to sizzle. Add 1/4 cup water. Cover tightly and reduce heat to low for 35 to 40 minutes. Makes 4 large servings.

Do not stir while cooking. Do not uncover during cooking time either.

MARINATED LONDON BROIL

1 1/2 lb. London broil
1/2 C. olive oil
1/2 C. red wine vinegar
1/4 C. teriyaki sauce
2 T. Worcestershire sauce
1 clove garlic, minced
2 tsp. dry mustard
1/2 tsp. freshly ground black pepper
Dash of cayenne pepper

Score meat on both sides in 1" squares. Put meat in 1 gallon Ziploc bag or large glass dish. Set aside. In a mixing bowl, combine remaining · ingredients, reserving 1/4 cup of mixture for basting. Pour other mixture over meat and marinate 8 hours in closed bag or covered dish in refrigerator. Turn several times during marinating. Remove the meat. Dispose of marinade. Grill over medium coals 6 to 8 minutes on each side. Baste with reserved marinade. Slice into thin slices across grain. Makes 6 servings.

MEAT LOAF IN A LOAF

1 loaf French or Italian bread
2 C. bread crumbs from loaf
1 2/3 C. evaporated milk
1 sm. onion, minced
1 1/2 lb. ground beef
1 sm. green pepper, minced
1 1/2 tsp. seasoned salt
1/2 tsp. pepper
Few dashes garlic salt
1 egg

Cut thin lengthwise slice from top of loaf; butter cut side of slice and set aside. Scoop out inside of bread, leaving a bread shell. Combine 2 cups of the bread crumbs with milk; let stand for 10 minutes. Add to all remaining ingredients. Pile into bread shell on baking sheet; bake at 350° for 1 hour. Put on top slice and bake an additional 5 minutes. Yield: 6 to 8 servings.

Unusual and pretty!

ONE-POT POT ROAST

4 lb. round or chuck beef roast
2 T. olive oil
1 can cream of mushroom soup
1 env. dry onion soup
1 C. water
6 or 7 potatoes, peeled and quartered
6 or 7 carrots, cut on the diagonal
   in 2" pieces

In a large, heavy pot, cook roast in hot oil, browning on all sides. Pour off fat and stir in mushroom soup, onion soup and water. Cover and simmer 2 hours, turning 2 or 3 times. Add vegetables and cook another 45 minutes to an hour. Remove roast and vegetables to serving platter. Thicken gravy as directed and serve over rice or roast and vegetables. Makes 8 servings.

Thickening for Gravy:

Dissolve 2 tablespoons all-purpose flour in 1/4 cup water and add to pan drippings.

SETTLER'S BEANS

2 lb. ground beef
1 onion, chopped
1/4 C. brown sugar
1 C. barbecue sauce
1 15-oz. can pork and beans
1 15-oz. can light kidney beans
1 15-oz. can great northern beans

Brown beef and onion; add other ingredients and simmer. (Do not drain beans.)

Ruby McCurry Matthews
(One of the Twelve)
Lincolnton, GA

SLOPPY JOE TURNOVERS

1 lb. ground beef
1/4 C. chopped onion
1/2 tsp. salt
1/4 tsp. garlic powder
1/2 C. catsup
1/4 C. dairy sour cream
10 oz. canned biscuits

Heat oven to 375°. In large skillet, brown ground beef and onions; drain. Add salt, garlic powder, catsup, and sour cream. Mix well. Roll out each biscuit into 4x4" square. Place 1/4 cup mixture on center of square. Fold over corner of square to form a triangle. Seal edges with fork and cut three 1/2" slices on top. Bake for 15 to 20 minutes or until golden brown.

Note: Brush with melted margarine if desired.

Betty Miller Wilkins
Prosperity, SC

SPAGHETTI SAUCE

1 onion, chopped
1 clove garlic
1 can tomato paste
1 jar marinara sauce
1 bell pepper, chopped
1 1/2 lb. ground beef
Salt and pepper, to taste

Brown onions; add bell pepper and garlic. Stir in ground beef with a fork to separate. Add salt and pepper. Add tomato paste and marinara sauce (rinse out can or jar with water as cooking takes up liquid). Cook slowly for several hours. Serve over cooked spaghetti. Add a little water if needed. Sprinkle Parmesan cheese over this and serve with tossed salad and garlic bread. Serves 4.

HORSERADISH CREAM SAUCE

4 T. freshly grated horseradish or
    2 T. prepared horseradish
1/4 tsp. onion juice
Few grains of cayenne pepper
1 1/2 T. vinegar
1/4 C. whipping cream (measured and
    then whipped until thick)

Mix all ingredients except whipped cream. Blend thoroughly and then fold in whipped cream. Chill and serve with roast beef or veal.

MARINADE

1 C. soy sauce
1/4 C. cream sherry
1 T. ground ginger
1 tsp. garlic powder or
    1 tsp. dried minced garlic
2 tsp. brown sugar

Mix well. Marinate 4 hours. Enough for 4 pounds meat.

May cut roast in 2x4" strips to marinate, then grill.

MARVELOUS MEAT MARINADE

1 C. soy sauce
1/2 C. olive oil
4 tsp. ground ginger
4 tsp. dry mustard
1/2 tsp. dried minced garlic or
   1 clove garlic, minced
1/2 tsp. pepper

Mix ingredients. Marinate in glass dish or plastic bag. Marinate meat for 5 to 6 hours. Keeps in refrigerator for 3 weeks.

Good marinade for any cut of beef. For London broil, grill 4 minutes on each side. Cool for 5 minutes, then slice diagonally.

TARRAGON SAUCE

1/2 C. Hellmann's mayonnaise
1/2 C. sour cream
2 T. lemon juice
1/4 tsp. dry mustard
1/4 tsp. garlic salt
1/2 tsp. tarragon

Place all ingredients in blender and blend until smooth.

Great on cold roast beef!

- PORK -

APRICOT GLACE PORK CHOPS

4 (1") pork chops
Salt and pepper
Flour
Oil
1 T. butter
1/2 C. apricot preserves
1 T. lemon juice

Season pork chops with salt and pepper; coat with flour and brown in oil. Place in shallow baking dish. Bake uncovered at 350° for 30 minutes. Combine remaining ingredients and spoon onto chops. Bake an additional 15 minutes. Yield: 4 servings.

Note: Pork chops may be stuffed with your favorite dressing after browning before baking in oven.

BAKED SPARERIBS

3 lb. spareribs
1 C. catsup
1/3 C. Worcestershire sauce
1 tsp. salt
1 tsp. chili powder
2 dashes Tabasco sauce
1 C. water
1 onion, thinly sliced
2 lemons, thinly sliced

Bake spareribs at 450° for 30 minutes; pour off fat. Combine catsup, Worcestershire sauce, salt, chili powder and Tabasco; add water and bring to a boil. Lay onion and lemon slices on top of spareribs. Pour sauce over ribs. Reduce heat to 350° and bake for 1 hour. Yield: 4 servings.

CABBAGE PATCH PORK (STIR-FRY)

2 T. peanut oil
1 tsp. salt
1 clove garlic
1/2 lb. fresh, uncooked lean pork,
    sliced in thin strips
2 tsp. soy sauce
1 tsp. MSG
1 tsp. sugar
1 tsp. sherry
2 lb. raw cabbage, finely shredded
1 1/2 C. chicken broth

Combine soy sauce, MSG, sugar and wine; set aside. Place oil in wok or skillet. Heat until oil begins to "smoke"; add salt and garlic; stir well. Add pork strips immediately and stir-fry until browning begins. Stir in soy sauce mixture and cook 1 minute, stirring all the while. Add shredded cabbage and stir-fry 3 to 4 minutes. Reduce heat to medium; add broth. Cover and cook for 3 to 5 minutes. Makes 2 to 4 servings.

CHARLESTON CHOPS

6 pork chops, center cut, 1/2" thick
Mustard
1/2 C. grated Parmesan cheese
2 tsp. rosemary, crushed
1 tsp. garlic salt

Coat chops on both sides with mustard. Sprinkle both sides with rosemary and garlic salt. Place in baking dish and top with Parmesan cheese. Bake at 350° for 40 minutes. Makes 6 servings.

GRILLED GLAZED RIBS

4 lb. country-style pork ribs,
    cut in serving pieces
1/4 C. corn syrup
1/2 C. spicy brown mustard
1/2 C. cider vinegar
1/4 C. lemon juice

Cook ribs in large pot with enough water to cover. Bring to a boil, reduce heat to a very low boil; cover and cook for 1 hour. In the meantime, mix glazing sauce: Syrup, mustard, vinegar and lemon juice; set aside. Drain ribs and baste with sauce. Grill about 5" from coals.

LEMON PORK CHOPS

6 boneless pork chops
1 T. margarine
6 lemon slices (approx. 1/4" thick)
1/2 C. ketchup
1/2 C. water
2 T. brown sugar

Brown pork chops on both sides in butter. Place in a shallow baking dish. Place 1 slice of lemon on each. Combine ketchup, water and brown sugar; pour over chops. Bake at 350° for 45 minutes. Makes 6 servings.

MARINATED PORK CHOPS

6 boneless pork chops, 1" thick
1 1/2 C. unsweetened pineapple juice
3/4 C. dry sherry
3 T. light brown sugar
1/2 tsp. crushed, dried rosemary
1 tsp. minced garlic
Sprinkle of red pepper flakes

Put pork chops in a heavy duty Ziploc bag or in a shallow glass dish. Set aside. Mix remaining ingredients; pour over chops. Seal bag or cover dish and refrigerate 12 to 24 hours. Remove chops from marinade. Broil 4½ to 6 minutes on each side, about 6" from heat. Makes 6 servings.

PEACH GLAZED PORK CHOPS

6 center-cut pork chops,
    cut 3/4 to 1" thick
1 clove garlic, minced
1 15-oz. can peach halves, drained
1/3 C. soy sauce
1/4 C. vegetable oil
1/4 C. honey
2 T. brown sugar
1/4 tsp. ground ginger

Sauce: Combine all ingredients except chops in blender or food processor until smooth (about 30 seconds). Bake, broil or grill pork chops. Baste with sauce on both sides last 15 minutes of cooking. Makes 6 servings.

PORK CHOP CASSEROLE

6 boneless (center cut) pork chops,
    browned, seasoned with
    salt and pepper
6 med. potatoes, peeled and
    sliced about 1/2" thick
1 sm. onion, peeled and sliced
1 can cream of mushroom soup
Salt and pepper, to taste

Place potatoes and onions in bottom of casserole dish; top with pork chops. Pour soup over all ingredients. Add salt and pepper liberally. Bake at 350° for 45 minutes. Serve with green salad and hot rolls.

QUICHE LORRAINE

4 eggs
1 10-oz. pkg. frozen Welsh Rarebit,
    defrosted
1/2 tsp. salt
1/4 tsp. pepper
5 slices bacon, fried and
    cut in 1" pieces
1 8" baked pie shell

Preheat oven to 350°. Beat eggs in a medium bowl; add defrosted Welsh Rarebit, salt and pepper; beat until well blended. Stir bacon pieces into mixture and pour into pie shell. Bake for 40 minutes or until a silver knife inserted in the center comes out clean. Cut into wedges and serve at once.

Note: To serve as hors d'oeuvres, bake the mixture in 16 prebaked tart shells for 30 to 35 minutes.

ROASTED PORK TENDERLOIN

5 to 6 lb. boneless whole
   pork tenderloin
2 tsp. salt
1 1/2 tsp. ground black pepper
   (1 tsp. freshly ground is best)
2 tsp. dried rosemary leaves

Place a piece of heavy duty aluminum foil in a large baking dish (enough foil to come up over sides of dish). Score any fat on roast with sharp knife. Combine salt, pepper and rosemary in a small bowl and mash together with the back of a teaspoon. Place pork, fat side up, in foil-lined baking dish. Rub liberally with salt mixture (add more if you like). Roast at 350° for 1½ to 1 3/4 hours. Slice and serve.

Note: Leftovers make good barbecue. Just slice thinly, add barbecue sauce and serve on sandwich buns.

SAUSAGE GRAVY & BISCUITS

3 C. self-rising soft wheat flour
1/4 tsp. baking soda
1 tsp. sugar
1/2 C. butter-flavored shortening
1 1/4 C. buttermilk
Butter or margarine, melted
Sausage Gravy

Combine first 3 ingredients in a large bowl; cut in shortening with a pastry blender until mixture is crumbly. Add buttermilk, stirring just until dry ingredients are moistened. Turn dough out onto a lightly floured surface, and knead lightly 4 to 5 times. Roll dough to 3/4" thickness; cut with a 2 1/2" biscuit cutter. Place on a lightly greased baking sheet. Bake at 425° for 12 to 14 minutes until golden. Brush tops with butter. Split biscuits open; serve with Sausage Gravy. Makes 12 to 14 servings.

Sausage Gravy:
1/2 lb. ground pork sausage
1/4 C. butter or margarine
1/3 C. all-purpose flour
3 1/4 C. 1% low-fat or whole milk
1/2 tsp. salt
1/2 tsp. pepper
1/8 tsp. Italian seasoning

Brown sausage in a skillet, stirring until it crumbles. Drain, reserving 1 tablespoon drippings in skillet. Set sausage aside. Add butter to drippings; heat over low heat until butter melts. Add flour, stirring until smooth. Cook 1 minute, stirring constantly. Gradually add milk; cook over medium heat, stirring constantly, until thickened and bubbly. Stir in seasonings and sausage. Cook until thoroughly heated, stirring constantly. Will make approximately 3 1/2 cups.

SAUSAGE SKILLET DINNER

1 lb. smoked sausage links
   (Hillshire Farm brand is best)
4 potatoes, sliced thin
1 green pepper, cut in small strips
4 carrots, sliced 1/3" thick
1 can French-style green beans,
   drained
1 onion, peeled and quartered
1 med. cabbage, cut in 8 wedges
Salt and pepper, to taste
1 to 1 1/2 C. water

Place sausage, sliced in 1" slices in bottom of large pot. Add other ingredients in order listed. Bring to a boil. Cover and reduce heat. Cook until vegetables are tender about 35 to 45 minutes. Makes 4 servings.

Smells wonderful; tastes great!

BAKED HAM

1 16-lb. whole smoked ham

Coating:
1 C. brown sugar
1 C. cornmeal
1 tsp. ground cloves
1 tsp. dry mustard

Place ham (skin side up) in roasting pan. Bake for 6 to 8 hours (or overnight) at 200°. Take ham from oven and remove skin and visible fat. Mix Coating ingredients together and rub on ham. Bake for 30 more minutes, uncovered, at 350°. Slice and serve.

Tender and tasty.

Flo Pursley
Lincolnton, GA

HAM BAKE CASSEROLE

2 C. cooked ham, cubed
2 C. cooked rice
1/2 C. grated American cheese
1/2 C. evaporated milk or light cream
1 10-oz. can cream of asparagus soup
4 T. chopped onion
3/4 C. crushed corn flakes
3 T. melted butter

Combine all ingredients except corn flakes and butter; place in lightly buttered casserole dish. Toss flakes with melted butter and sprinkle over casserole. Bake uncovered at 375° for 20 to 25 minutes until top is lightly brown. If desired, garnish with a pinwheel of hot, cooked asparagus tips. Yield: 6 servings.

Good use for leftovers.

MARYETTA'S SUGAR CURED HAM (HAM WHAT AM)

1 fattened hog (freshly killed),
   cut into hams, bacon, etc.
4 lb. light brown sugar
8 lb. white salt
2 T. saltpeter
2 T. black pepper, coarsely ground

Select shoulders and hams to be sugar cured. Combine remaining ingredients and rub into meat (while meat is still warm . . . as in just killed, not just cooked). Wrap in brown paper. Rub mixture in several more times. Place ham, joint end down, in a white cloth sack and hang to cure. Takes about 6 weeks. Slice, soak in cold water 1/2 hour, drain and fry.

There's nothing like it! This recipe is almost a hundred years old.

Aunt Joann McCurry Ferguson &
Uncle Hammond Ferguson
Lincolnton, GA

SWEET POTATO/HAM BAKE

1 lb. slice of ham
2 med. sweet potatoes, peeled
2 T. brown sugar
1/2 tsp. ground cinnamon
1 C. hot water

Cut ham in 4 equal pieces; brown slightly in skillet, then place ham into glass baking dish. Slice the sweet potatoes 1/2" thick; place on top of ham; sprinkle with sugar and cinnamon. Add hot water to pan drippings; pour over sweet potatoes. Cover with foil and bake for 30 minutes at 350° , basting occasionally. Remove cover and bake for 15 minutes more. Makes 4 servings.

DILLED MUSTARD SAUCE

3 T. brown mustard
3 T. cider vinegar
2 T. sugar
2/3 C. vegetable oil
1/2 tsp. dried dillweed

Combine all ingredients; place in a covered jar or covered cruet and shake well to blend. Makes 1 cup.

Delicious with ham or any kind of fish.

PINEAPPLE SALSA

1 8-oz. can crushed pineapple, drained
1/4 C. chopped green or
   red sweet pepper
2 T. minced onion
1 sm. jalapeno pepper,
   seeded and minced
1 T. lemon juice
1 tsp. honey
2 T. finely chopped, fresh cilantro or
   fresh mint

Combine pineapple, sweet pepper, onion, jalapeno pepper, lemon juice and honey. Mix well; cover and refrigerate for 1 hour.

When ready to serve, stir in cilantro or mint. Great with grilled pork, ham or chicken!

Cakes & Pies

- CAKES -

APRICOT NECTAR CAKE

1 bx. vanilla flavored cake mix or
   yellow cake mix
4 eggs, separated*
3/4 C. Wesson oil
3/4 C. apricot nectar
1 1/2 tsp. lemon extract
1/2 tsp. vanilla

*Reserve egg whites in a glass bowl; beat 3 to 4 minutes until stiff but not dry.

Combine cake mix, egg yolks, Wesson oil, apricot nectar, lemon extract and vanilla. Fold in beaten egg whites. Pour into slightly buttered or greased Bundt or tube pan (or spray with Baker's Joy or Pam). Bake for 1 hour at 325°. Cool for 5 minutes. Punch holes in cake with ice pick or wooden skewer. Pour Glaze over cake. Cake will absorb Glaze while cooling.

Glaze:
1 1/2 C. powdered sugar
Juice and grated rind of 2 lemons

Mix together. Pour over cake. Garnish with pieces of lemon made with lemon "zester".

Beth's favorite.

BEER CAKE & ICING

2 C. brown sugar
1 C. margarine
2 eggs, beaten
2 C. beer
3 C. flour
Pinch of salt
1/2 tsp. cloves
2 tsp. soda
2 tsp. allspice
2 tsp. cinnamon
1 C. nuts, chopped
2 C. dates, chopped

Cream shortening and sugar; add eggs and beat well. Sift 2 1/2 cups flour, salt, soda and spices. Alternate dry ingredients and beer. Mix nuts and dates with remaining 1/2 cup flour. Fold into batter. Bake in slightly greased tube pan for 1 hour at 350°.

Icing:
1 8-oz. pkg. Philadelphia cream
   cheese, room temperature
1/4 lb. butter or margarine,
   room temperature
1 lb. powdered sugar
1 tsp. vanilla
1 C. chopped pecans

Blend cream cheese, butter or margarine and powdered sugar. Add vanilla and pecans. Put on cake while still warm.

CAST IRON CAKE

1 qt. chopped pecans
2 bx. dates, chopped
2 7-oz. cans shredded coconut
2 14-oz. cans sweetened
    condensed milk

Place all ingredients in a large mixing bowl; stir until well blended. Pour into well-greased 10" cast iron skillet. Bake at 350° for 1 hour. Cool in pan, then invert pan on cake plate to remove cake.

Wonderful topped with whipped cream!

CHEWY FUDGE "CARAMEL CAKE"

1 1/2 C. all-purpose flour
1 C. sifted cornstarch
1 T. baking powder
2 C. butter or margarine
2 C. granulated sugar
1 C. milk
7 egg whites
1 recipe Chewy Fudge Frosting

Grease and lightly flour two 9x1½" round cake pans or one 13x9x2" baking pan; set aside. Stir together flour, cornstarch, and baking powder. Set aside. In large mixer bowl, beat butter or margarine on medium speed of electric mixer about 30 seconds. Add the granulated sugar; beat until well combined. Alternately add dry ingredients and the 1 cup milk, beating on low speed after each addition until just combined. Transfer batter to a large mixing bowl. Wash beaters. In another bowl, beat egg whites until stiff peaks form (tips stand straight). Fold into batter until combined. Turn batter into prepared pan(s). Bake in 350° oven for 25 to 30 minutes for the 9x1½" pans or 40 to 45 minutes for the 13x9x2" pan. Cool on wire rack for 10 minutes. Remove from pan. Cool thoroughly. Pour frosting over cake. Serves 12.

Chewy Fudge Frosting:
1/2 C. butter or margarine
1 C. packed brown sugar
1/2 C. milk
2 squares (2-oz.) unsweetened
    chocolate, cut up
2 T. light cream or milk
2 tsp. vanilla

In heavy 1½-quart saucepan, melt the butter or margarine. Add sugar; stir thoroughly. Add the 1/2 cup milk and chocolate; stir constantly until mixture boils. Cook over medium heat, stirring occasionally, to 245° (firm ball stage), 20 to 30 minutes (mixture should boil gently over surface). Remove from heat; stir in cream and vanilla. Quickly pour and spread on cake.

CHOCOLATE COVERED CHERRY CAKE

1 bx. Duncan Hines fudge cake mix
   (mix with oil directions)
1 can cherry pie filling

    Mix cake as directed, using oil instead of margarine. Fold in can of cherry pie filling. Bake for 30 to 35 minutes in oblong baking pan. While warm, top with Fudge Icing.

Fudge Icing:
1 stick margarine
1 tsp. vanilla
3 T. cocoa
1 bx. confectioner's 4X sugar
2 T. to 1/4 C. milk

    Bring margarine, vanilla and cocoa to a boil. Add sugar and milk. Beat with hand mixer until creamy. Spread on top of warm cake.

Sara Winn
Manchester, GA

CRAZY CAKE

1 bx. German chocolate cake mix
1 stick butter
1 egg, beaten
1 C. chopped nuts
1 8-oz. pkg. cream cheese, softened
1 bx. powdered sugar
2 eggs, beaten for 3 minutes

    Mix first 4 ingredients together. This will be stiff. Spread mixture evenly into a greased and floured 9x13" pan. Mix last 3 ingredients together and pour over cake mixture. Bake at 350° for 35 to 45 minutes. Cool and slice into 12 squares. Makes 12 servings.

SARA'S GERMAN CHOCOLATE CAKE (UP-SIDE DOWN)

1 bx. German chocolate cake mix
   (mixed as directed)
2 8-oz. bags frozen coconut, thawed
1 C. chopped pecans
1 stick butter
8 oz. cream cheese
1 bx. confectioner's sugar

    Grease and flour a 9x13" baking dish. Place coconut and pecans in bottom. Mix cake as directed and pour over top of coconut and pecans. In a saucepan, combine butter and cream cheese. Melt over medium heat. Add powdered sugar. Mix well and pour over cake mix. Bake for 30 to 40 minutes in preheated 350° oven. Will not look done, but is. Cool and cut in squares to serve.

Sara Winn
Manchester, GA

SOUTHERN HOT COCOA CAKE

1 stick butter or margarine
3 T. oil
1 C. water
3 T. cocoa
2 C. self-rising flour
2 C. sugar
1/2 C. buttermilk
1/2 tsp. cinnamon
1 tsp. vanilla
2 beaten eggs

Combine first 4 ingredients and bring to a boil. Stir in flour and sugar. Add and mix well the buttermilk, cinnamon, vanilla and beaten eggs. Pour into greased and floured 9x13" pan. Bake at 350° for 30 to 40 minutes.

Frosting:
1/2 stick butter or margarine
1 T. cocoa
6 T. milk
1/2 bx. 4X sugar
1/2 C. pecans
1 tsp. vanilla

Mix well and spread on cake while warm.

PLANTATION COCONUT CAKE

1 C. shortening
2 C. granulated sugar
5 eggs, beaten
1 C. all-purpose flour
1 C. self-rising flour
1 C. milk
1 tsp. vanilla

Using an electric mixer, cream shortening and sugar together in a large mixing bowl; add beaten eggs. Sift all-purpose and self-rising flour together. Add flour to sugar, shortening and eggs (a little at a time). Stir in milk and vanilla. Mix until well blended. Pour into 2 greased and floured cake pans. Bake at 350° for 25 to 30 minutes. Cool slightly and frost. Store in refrigerator in airtight container.

Uncooked Coconut Frosting:
2 C. granulated sugar
1 C. sour cream
1 12-oz. pkg. frozen coconut
1 tsp. lemon juice

Mix all ingredients. Spread between warm cake layers, top and sides.

DUMP CAKE ALICE

1 21-oz. can cherry pie filling
1 17-oz. can crushed pineapple
  (do not drain)
1 yellow cake mix
3/4 C. butter, cut in small pieces
1 C. shredded coconut
1 C. chopped pecans

Place ingredients in order listed into a large greased 9x13" baking dish. Bake at 325° for 1 hour. Top with Cool Whip if desired.
Easy and delicious.

Alice Plemons
Manchester, GA

HEATH BAR CAKE

1/2 C. butter
2 C. flour
2 C. brown sugar
1 C. milk
1 egg
1 tsp. soda
Pinch of salt
1/2 C. chopped nuts
6 Heath candy bars, chopped

Cut butter into flour and sugar. Reserve 1 cup for topping. To the remaining mixture, add milk, egg, soda and salt. Pour into greased Bundt pan. Mix reserved flour/sugar mixture with nuts and chopped candy bars. Pour on top of cake. Bake at 350° for 30 to 40 minutes. Cool slightly. Invert cake onto plate.

Delicious!

GRACE'S LEMON CHEESE CAKE AND FILLING

2 C. granulated sugar
1/2 C. butter
3/4 C. whole milk
Whites of 6 eggs, beaten stiff
1/4 tsp. salt
3 C. plain flour
3 tsp. baking powder

Cream butter and sugar. Sift flour, baking powder and salt together, then add alternately with milk to butter mixture. Fold in beaten egg whites last. Bake in 3 greased and floured cake pans at 375° about 25 minutes. If cake springs back after light pressure, it's done. Cool layers on wire rack.

Filling:
Grated rind and juice of 2 lemons
Yolks of 3 eggs
1/2 C. butter
1 C. granulated sugar

Mix all ingredients together in a saucepan. Cook until thick, stirring all the while. Spread between and on top and sides of layers.

This recipe is over 100 years old.

Grace Booker Radford
Dawson, GA

MEETING STREET CAKE

1/2 C. margarine
1 C. granulated sugar
1 C. self-rising flour
1/2 C. milk
1 can pie filling (any kind)
Vanilla ice cream

Melt margarine in baking dish. Mix flour, sugar and milk together. Pour over melted margarine. Pour pie filling over flour mixture. Do not stir! Bake at 350° for 40 minutes. Top with vanilla ice cream.

Enjoy!

ORANGE SLICE CAKE

1 C. butter
2 C. sugar
1 C. buttermilk
3 C. plain flour
2 T. molasses
1 tsp. soda
1/2 tsp. ground cloves
2 tsp. ground cinnamon
2 tsp. ground allspice
2 tsp. ground nutmeg
4 eggs
2 tsp. baking powder

Filling:
2 C. sugar
2 eggs, beaten
2 lg. oranges (juice and grated rind)
1/2 C. cold water
2 tsp. cornstarch
1 T. butter
1 C. boiling water

Sift spices, soda and baking powder with flour. Cream butter and sugar; add beaten eggs and liquid (molasses and milk). Bake in 3 layers in a moderate oven.

Mix sugar, beaten eggs, orange juice and rind. Pour in boiling water. Add cornstarch dissolved in cold water. Add butter and cook until thickens. Cool. When cold, spread between layers.

Frost with favorite "puffy" frosting. Regular 7 Minute Frosting will do.

Very old recipe.

Maryetta Ferguson
(Uncle Hammond's Mother)
Lincolnton, GA

PINEAPPLE CAKE

1 C. butter, softened
2 C. granulated sugar
4 eggs (yolks and whites separated)
3 C. plain flour
1 1/2 tsp. baking powder
1 tsp. salt
1 1/4 C. whole milk

Beat egg whites until stiff; set aside. Beat yolks until foamy; set aside. In mixing bowl, cream butter and sugar; add egg yolks. Beat well. Sift flour, baking powder and salt together. Add flour mixture and milk alternately with butter mixture. Fold in beaten egg whites. Pour mixture evenly into 3 greased and buttered cake pans. Bake for 35 to 40 minutes at 400°.

Filling:
1 lg. can crushed pineapple
1 C. sugar
2 T. flour
2 T. butter

Drain pineapple (reserve juice). In a saucepan, combine sugar, flour and butter with juice. Cook until thick; add pineapple and spread on hot cake layers, top and sides.

EASY PLUM CAKE

2 C. sugar
3/4 C. Wesson oil
3 eggs
2 sm. jars plum baby food
    (I use 1 plum and 1 apricot)
2 C. self-rising flour
1 tsp. cloves
1 tsp. cinnamon
1 1/2 C. nuts

Mix all ingredients together except nuts (save some flour for nuts). Mix for about 4 minutes. Flour nuts and add. Stir. Bake in a greased tube or Bundt pan for 1 hour at 325°. Cool 10 minutes.

Plum good!

Lynda Rogers
Manchester, GA

POPPY SEED BREAD (CAKE)

1 pkg. yellow cake mix (dry)
1 1/2 pkg. instant butterscotch
    pudding (no cook kind)
4 eggs, beaten
1/4 C. cooking oil
1 C. water
1 sm. can poppy seeds
Powdered sugar

Mix all ingredients in a large bowl and pour into 2 greased loaf pans. Bake at 350° for 45 minutes. Dust top with powdered sugar. Makes 2 loaves.

Alice was the best neighbor anyone could have!

Alice Plemons
Manchester, GA (1976)

PRALINE CAKE SQUARES

1 C. buttermilk
1/2 C. (1 stick) butter
2 C. brown sugar
2 eggs
1 tsp. baking soda
2 C. plain flour
2 rounded T. cocoa
1 T. vanilla

In a saucepan, heat buttermilk and butter until butter melts. Pour into mixing bowl. Using the mixer, add brown sugar and eggs. Beat well. Sift dry ingredients together and add to mixture. Add vanilla; mix. Pour into greased and floured 9x13" baking pan (at least 2" deep). Bake at 350° for 20 to 25 minutes.

Icing:
1 stick margarine, softened
6 T. evaporated milk
1 C. brown sugar
1 C. chopped pecans

While cake is baking, mix ingredients in a bowl. As soon as cake is done, spread Icing on top. Turn oven to broil. Place cake on bottom rack and broil only until Icing bubbles. Watch carefully. As soon as Icing bubbles, remove from oven. Cool slightly. Crust in squares and serve.

- POUND CAKES -

ALMOND POUND CAKE

2 C. all-purpose flour
2 C. granulated sugar
1 C. vegetable oil
6 eggs
2 T. almond flavoring

Combine oil and sugar; mix well. Alternately add flour and eggs. Add flavoring. Bake in a lightly greased tube or Bundt pans at 325° for 1 hour 15 minutes. Makes 12 to 16 servings.

AUNT GLENNIE'S POUND CAKE

1 C. butter
3 C. sifted Swan's Down cake flour
3 C. sugar
1 C. less 1 T. evaporated milk
6 eggs
1/2 tsp. vanilla extract
1/2 tsp. almond extract
Dash nutmeg (fresh ground is best)

Cream butter and sugar. Add eggs, one at a time. Add flour and milk alternately. Add vanilla, almond and nutmeg. Start baking in a cold oven in a greased and floured Bundt or tube pan. Set oven to 300° and bake for 1 hour 25 minutes. Makes 24 servings.

Aunt Glennie uses loaf pans too. Great with strawberries and whipped cream.

Glennie McCurry Norman
(One of the Twelve)
Thomson, GA

AUNT JOANN'S POUND CAKE

1 1/2 C. butter
2 C. granulated sugar
7 eggs
3 C. all-purpose flour
1/2 tsp. vanilla
1/2 tsp. fresh lemon juice

Mix sugar and butter until well blended. Add 1 egg at a time, beating well after each egg is added. Add vanilla and lemon juice. Add flour, 1 cup at a time on low speed until all flour is used. Bake at 300° for 1 hour 15 minutes.

Joann McCurry Ferguson
(One of the Twelve)
Lincolnton, GA

BETTY'S BUTTERNUT POUND CAKE

2 sticks butter or margarine
3 C. granulated sugar
1/2 C. Crisco
5 lg. eggs
3 1/4 C. all-purpose flour
1 sm. can evaporated milk (add
    enough to water to make
    1 C. liquid)
1/4 tsp. salt
2 T. butternut flavoring

Cream butter and shortening with sugar and salt. Add eggs, 1 at a time. Add flour and milk alternately. Fold in flavoring. Bake in greased tube or Bundt pan at 300° for 1 hour 20 minutes. (Start in cold oven.) Makes 16 servings.

Betty Miller Wilkins
Prosperity, SC

COCONUT POUND CAKE

3 C. plain or cake flour
1 tsp. salt
1 tsp. baking powder
1 C. milk
1 1/2 C. Crisco
2 1/2 C. sugar
5 eggs
1 C. coconut
1 tsp. vanilla or almond flavoring

Sift flour, baking powder and salt. Cream shortening (or margarine) and sugar. Add eggs, 1 at a time; add flour alternately with milk. Add flavoring and coconut. Put in greased tube pan. Put in cold oven, then bake at 325° for 1 hour and 25 minutes. Let cool in pan for 20 minutes before turning out.
    Good toasted!

NANNIE'S LEMON POUND CAKE

1 bx. yellow or lemon cake mix
1 C. water
1/3 C. Crisco oil
4 eggs
1 bx. lemon Jell-O

Mix well for 2 minutes. Pour into greased tube or Bundt cake pan. Bake for 40 to 45minutes in 350° preheated oven. As soon as cake is removed from the oven, punch holes in top of cake with a fork. (Cake is still in pan.) Mix together 1/3 cup lemon juice and 1/3 cup sugar. Pour over cake (will seep into holes). Let cake cool in pan for 10 to 20 minutes and turn out onto plate. Use drizzle icing on top or sprinkle with powdered sugar.
    Nannie's recipe came from Donnie Edmunds Rector of Kingsport, TN.

Donnie Edmunds Rector
Kingsport, TN

- FILLINGS & FROSTINGS, ETC. -

LEMON FILLING

1 lb. granulated sugar
1/4 lb. butter
6 eggs
Grated rind of 2 lemons
Juice of 3 lemons

Combine all ingredients in a double boiler and cook over hot water until it is the consistency of custard.

Keeps indefinitely and is wonderful to have in reserve.

Filling for cakes or tarts.

Thelma Hammond
Lincolnton, GA

SARA'S LEMON CHEESE FILLING

1 C. sugar
3 T. cornstarch
2 whole lemons (juice and
    grated rinds)
1 C. water
1/2 stick margarine, melted
2 egg yolks

Beat egg yolks with a little of the sugar. Mix sugar, egg yolks, water, margarine, lemon juice, grated lemon rind and cornstarch. Cook over medium heat until thick. Cool before putting on cake. Frosts 3 layers; sides and tops.

Sara Winn
Manchester, GA

CHOCOLATE FROSTING

2 squares unsweetened chocolate
2/3 C. milk
1/2 tsp. salt
2 C. sugar
1/2 C. vegetable shortening
2 tsp. vanilla

Place all ingredients except vanilla in a pan. Bring to a boil and boil for 1 minute. Remove from fire and beat until lukewarm. Add vanilla. Beat until hard enough to spread. Add 1 teaspoon cream if icing is too hard.

LILLIAN'S CHOCOLATE NUT ICING

2 C. granulated sugar
1 stick butter, cut in 8 pieces
3 T. cocoa
3/4 C. evaporated milk
1 C. chopped nuts

In a saucepan, stir sugar and cocoa together. Add butter and milk. Cook and stir over medium heat until butter melts and mixture bubbles. Then reduce heat to low and cook 6 to 8 minutes. Remove from heat; mix with hand mixer until glaze appears. Fold in chopped nuts. Add a little more evaporated milk if icing is too hard.

Lillian Radford
Dawson, GA

PEANUT BUTTER FROSTING

1/4 C. milk, heated
1/4 C. peanut butter
2 T. butter, softened
1/2 C. light brown sugar
1/2 tsp. vanilla

Using electric mixer, combine the ingredients until smooth. Then gradually add 1 1/2 cups confectioner's sugar. Frosts two 8" layers or 1 dozen cupcakes.

SEVEN MINUTE FROSTING

7/8 C. sugar, granulated
3 T. water
1 egg white
1 tsp. vanilla

Combine ingredients in top of double boiler over boiling water. Using hand mixer, beat at high speed for 7 minute. Remove from heat. Add vanilla and spread between layers and on top and sides of cake.
Foolproof!

CHOCOLATE LEAVES

8 oz. semi-sweet chocolate
1 T. vegetable shortening
Camellia or any waxy plant leaves

Melt chocolate and shortening together in top of double boiler. Using a tablespoon, generously coat the underside of clean, dry leaves. Place on a wax paper-lined cookie sheet in a single layer and chill or freeze until firm, then peel off leaves.

You'll have perfect chocolate leaves for garnishing pies, cakes. etc.

- PIES -

"EASY AS PIE" APPLE PIE

1 9" unbaked pie shell
1 20-oz. can Thank You brand
    sliced apples (original)
1/2 C. granulated sugar
1/2 C. brown sugar
1/4 tsp. salt
3/4 tsp. cinnamon
1/4 tsp. nutmeg

Topping:
1/4 C. granulated sugar
1/4 tsp. salt
1 stick butter
1 C. all-purpose flour

Pour apples into unbaked pie crust. Mix sugar and spices together; sprinkle over apples.

In a mixing bowl, combine all ingredients, cutting in butter with a pastry blender until crumbly. Sprinkle over apples and spices. Bake at 450° for 10 minutes, then at 375° for 40 to 50 minutes. Makes 6 to 8 servings.

Serve very warm. Good reheated with a slice of Cheddar cheese melted on top of each slice.

CANDY BAR PIE

6 (1.5-oz.) Hershey's almond bars
1 9-oz. ctn. Cool Whip
1 baked 9" pastry pie shell or
    1 9" graham cracker crust
Slivered almonds

Melt candy bars in top of double boiler over hot water. Add Cool Whip; pour into pie shell and top with slivered almonds. Refrigerate at least 6 hours or overnight. Slice and serve.

Delicious!

COMPANY CHOCOLATE PIE

1 1/2 C. granulated sugar
1/2 C. cornstarch
1/2 C. cocoa
1/4 tsp. salt
3 egg yolks
2 1/2 C. milk
1/2 tsp. vanilla
1 baked pie shell
Whipped cream, for garnish

Bake pie shell. Mix sugar, cornstarch, cocoa and salt together. Add a 1/2 cup of milk and egg yolks. Blend these ingredients well. Add remaining 2 cups of milk. Pour into top of double boiler over hot water, stirring occasionally, and cook until mixture is thick. Add vanilla. Cool, then pour into baked pie shell. Chill and top with whipped cream. Makes 6 to 8 servings.

COCONUT PIE

1 cooked 9" pie shell
3/4 C. sugar
2 heaping T. plain flour
1 C. coconut
1 1/4 C. milk
3 eggs, beaten
1/2 tsp. vanilla
1 tsp. butter

Mix together sugar, flour and coconut. Combine milk, eggs, vanilla and butter over low heat; add the sugar mixture and cook until thickened. Pour into cooked pie shell. Bake at 350° for 15 to 20 minutes. Cool.

Lynda Rogers
Manchester, GA

DOUGH FOR FRIED PIES

3 C. all-purpose flour
1 C. Crisco
1 beaten egg (beaten in
    measuring cup with enough water
    to make 1/2 C.)
1 tsp. salt

Cut Crisco into flour with pastry blender. Add beaten egg, water and salt. Mix well. Form into ball. On a lightly floured surface, roll out 1/4" thick; cut in 5" circles. Place 1 tablespoon cooked, dried fruit in center. Fold dough over fruit to form half circle. Seal edges with water.

SOUTHERN FRIED FRUIT PIES

2 C. plain flour
1/2 tsp. salt
1 tsp. soda
1/2 C. shortening
4 T. cold water
1 T. vinegar
Dried fruit of choice, cooked as
    per directions and cooled

Mix all ingredients except fruit in the order they appear in recipe. Cut in shortening with fork and knead mixture 3 or 4 times. Place in covered bowl. Refrigerate for 2 or more hours. Roll out chilled pastry on floured surface until 1/4" thick. Cut into 5" in diameter circles. Place fruit mixture in center of circle; fold pastry over fruit, sealing edges with a little water, then press around edge with tines of fork. Fry in hot oil (enough to cover pies) for approximately 1 to 2 minutes each. Remove from oil; drain on paper towels. Dust with granulated sugar.
A real treat!

FRUIT PIES (ANY KIND)

Any flavor canned pie filling
2 unbaked 9" pie shells
1 8-oz. pkg. cream cheese
1 sm. ctn. Cool Whip
1 C. pecans, chopped
1 C. 4X powdered sugar

Place nuts on bottom of pie shells and bake according to package directions. Let cool completely. Combine cream cheese, sugar and Cool Whip. Pour this mixture over nuts in pie shells. Top with any canned pie filling. Makes two 9" pies.

GRAPE-NUTS PIE

1/2 C. Grape-Nuts cereal
1/2 C. lukewarm water
1 C. firmly packed brown sugar
1 C. dark corn syrup
1/4 C. butter
3 eggs
1/8 tsp. salt
1 tsp. vanilla
1 unbaked pie shell

Put Grape-Nuts in lukewarm water. Set aside until water is absorbed. In a saucepan, combine sugar, syrup, butter and salt. Bring to boil, stirring, until sugar is dissolved. Remove from heat. Beat eggs until foamy. Add small amount of hot mixture to eggs, mixing well. Stir in softened Grape-Nuts and vanilla. Pour into unbaked pie shell. Bake at 375° for 45 to 50 minutes. Garnish with whipped cream. Makes 6 to 8 servings.

A very old recipe! Good for you, too.

GEORGIA GRASSHOPPER PIE

14 chocolate sandwich cookies,
    crushed
2 T. butter, melted
24 lg. marshmallows
1/2 C. milk
4 T. creme de menthe
2 T. white creme de cacao
1 C. whipping cream, whipped

Combine cookies and butter; press into bottom and sides of 8" pie pan and chill. Combine marshmallows and milk in top of double boiler; heat until marshmallows are melted. Remove from heat and cool. Add liqueurs and fold in whipped cream. Pour into pie shell and freeze. Garnish with Chocolate Leaves (see Table of Contents).

GRITS AND COCONUT PIE

1/3 C. yellow grits
1/4 tsp. salt
1 1/2 C. boiling water
2/3 C. brown sugar
1 1/3 C. evaporated milk
3 eggs, slightly beaten
1 tsp. vanilla
1 C. coconut (canned or frozen)
1 unbaked 9" pie crust

In a large mixing bowl, stir together grits, boiling water and salt; stir in remaining ingredients. Mix for about 1 minute and pour mixture into unbaked pie crust. Bake in preheated 325° oven for 1 hour. Makes 6 servings.

LEMON CHESS PIE

1/2 stick butter, softened
1 C. sugar
3 eggs, beaten
1 tsp. flour
2 tsp. cornmeal
1 T. milk
1/4 C. lemon juice
1/2 tsp. grated lemon rind
1 can blueberry pie filling, heated
Partially baked 9" pie shell

Cream butter and sugar. Add beaten eggs, milk, cornmeal and flour. Mix until smooth (use hand mixer). Add lemon juice and rind. Pour into partially baked pie shell and bake at 350° for 30 minutes. Top with heated blueberry pie filling.

LEMON ICEBOX PIE

1 can sweetened condensed milk
Juice of 3 lemons
3 egg yolks (reserve whites
    for Meringue)
3 T. granulated sugar
Grated rind of 1 lemon
1 9" graham cracker crust

Combine beaten egg yolks with milk and lemon juice. Stir well until thick. Add sugar and grated lemon rind. Mix and pour into graham cracker crust. Top with Meringue.

Meringue:
3 egg whites
2 T. granulated sugar
1/8 tsp. cornstarch
Tiny pinch of salt

Beat egg whites until frothy; add sugar and cornstarch. Beat until stiff. Pile on pie. Bake at 325° until lightly browned. Cool and refrigerate for 4 to 6 hours before serving. Makes 6 to 8 servings.
Very rich.

Lillian Radford
Dawson, GA

LITTLE MARY'S LEMON MERINGUE PIE

1 9" graham cracker crust
1 15-oz. can Eagle Brand sweetened
    condensed milk
2 eggs, separated
1/2 C. lemon juice (fresh or bottled)
1/4 tsp. lemon extract
1/4 C. sugar (for meringue)

Blend milk and egg yolks. Gradually add juice and extract, stirring until well blended. Pour into crust.
Meringue: Whip egg whites; gradually add sugar until stiff, but not dry. Place on filling, sealing to crust. Bake at 325° until brown, about 15 minutes. Cool and refrigerate for 3 to 4 hours before serving. Makes 6 to 8 servings.

Betty Miller Wilkins
Prosperity, SC

LEMON PIE

4 eggs
Pinch of salt
1 1/2 T. butter
2 level C. sugar
2 lg. lemons (use juice and grated rind)
1 unbaked pie shell
Whipped cream

In a mixing bowl, beat eggs, using whisk, just slightly. Melt butter until it begins to brown. Pour into eggs. Add remaining ingredients. Beat with whisk until smooth. Pour into unbaked pie shell. Bake at 300° for 45 minutes. Cool and top with sweetened, whipped cream. Makes 6 to 8 servings.

KEY LIME PIE

1 14-oz. can Eagle Brand
   condensed milk
1/3 C. fresh lime juice
1/2 tsp. finely grated lime peel
3 egg yolks, beaten
3 egg whites, beaten stiff
1 9" baked pie shell

Combine condensed milk, lime juice and grated peel and well-beaten egg yolks. Mix well and fold in stiffly beaten egg whites. Pour into baked pie shell. Bake at 250° for 10 minutes. Cool and refrigerate for at least 3 hours before serving.

FUZZY NAVEL PIE

1 14-oz. can sweetened
   condensed milk
2 cans Mandarin orange sections,
   drained (save several for garnish)
2 tsp. grated orange rind
1 C. pecans or almonds,
   chopped, toasted
1 10-oz. ctn. Cool Whip
1/2 C. lemon juice
2 T. peach schnapps
2 9" graham cracker crusts

Combine first 7 ingredients in a large mixing bowl. Pour into graham cracker crusts. Garnish with orange sections. Cover and refrigerate. Makes 12 to 14 servings (2 pies).

PEANUT BUTTER ICE CREAM PIE

1 graham cracker pie crust
1 qt. vanilla ice cream
1 C. crunchy peanut butter
Roasted peanuts and chocolate curls,
   for garnish

Thaw ice cream and place it in a mixing bowl with peanut butter; mix thoroughly. Pour into pie crust, cover and freeze. Serve frozen. Garnish with roasted peanuts and chocolate curls. Serves 8.

Note: Chocolate curls are easily made by using a potato peeler dipped in hot water and drawn over a block of chocolate or a plain chocolate candy bar.

FROZEN PEANUT BUTTER PIE

1 9" graham cracker crust
1/2 C. smooth peanut butter
8 oz. softened cream cheese
1 C. 10X powdered sugar
1/2 C. milk
1 med. ctn. Cool Whip, thawed
Shaved chocolate and chopped
   salted peanuts, for garnish

In a large mixing bowl, cream together peanut butter, cream cheese and sugar. Gradually add milk, stirring until smooth, then add Cool Whip. Mix well and pour into pie shell. Garnish with shaved chocolate and chopped nuts. Freeze for at least 3 hours, covered. Remove from freezer 45 minutes before serving. Makes 6 to 8 servings.

Easy and wonderfully delicious!

PECAN FUDGE PIE

4 tsp. cocoa
1/2 C. butter or margarine
1 C. granulated sugar
2 eggs, beaten
Pinch of salt
1/2 C. self-rising flour
1 tsp. vanilla
1 C. pecan halves

Melt cocoa in butter. Add beaten eggs and remaining ingredients. Mix well. Pour into a greased pie pan and bake at 350° for 30 to 35 minutes. Garnish with whipped cream or a scoop of ice cream.

Florie McCurry Edmunds
(One of the Twelve)
Lincolnton, GA

SOUTHERN PECAN PIE

2 C. white corn syrup (Karo)
1 C. sugar
2 sticks butter or margarine
6 eggs, beaten
2 C. pecans
2 unbaked pie shells

Boil together syrup, sugar and butter. In a mixing bowl, beat eggs and pour hot syrup into eggs, beating all the while. Divide into 2 unbaked pie shells and place 1 cup of pecans in each. Bake at 350° for 20 minutes, then 15 minutes at 400°. Makes 2 pies (16 servings).

Great with scoop of vanilla ice cream on each slice when serving.

RUM RAISIN PIE

1 C. granulated sugar
1/2 tsp. ground cinnamon
1/2 tsp. ground cloves
2 eggs, beaten
1 C. seedless raisins
1 C. sour cream
Pinch of salt
2 T. white vinegar
1 tsp. rum flavoring (optional)
1 baked 9" pie shell

Mix ingredients together, stirring until sugar is dissolved. Pour into baked pie shell. Bake in 350° preheated oven for 25 to 30 minutes. Makes 6 servings.

Garnish with whipped cream.

SUMMER STRAWBERRY PIE

1 graham cracker pie shell
1 C. granulated sugar
3 T. strawberry Jell-O
3 T. cornstarch
1 C. water
2 C. (approx. 1 pt.) sliced strawberries
    (reserve a few whole for garnish)
Whipped cream or Cool Whip

In a saucepan, mix sugar, Jell-O, cornstarch and water and bring to a rolling boil. Cool. Place sliced strawberries in graham cracker crust. Pour Jell-O mixture over strawberries, cover and place in refrigerator until chilled and set. Top each slice with whipped cream or Cool Whip.

Candies, Cookies
&
Brownies

- CANDIES -

BUTTERSCOTCH CLUSTERS

1 sm. pkg. butterscotch pudding mix
1 C. granulated sugar
1 T. butter
1/2 C. evaporated milk
1 1/2 C. chopped nuts

In a saucepan, mix pudding powder, sugar, butter and milk. Cook over medium heat, stirring until soft ball stage (when a drop or two placed in cold water forms a soft ball). Remove from heat and cool slightly. Beat until mixture starts to thicken. Fold in nuts and drop from teaspoon onto wax paper. Makes 2 dozen.

TERESA'S CHOCOLATE COVERED CHERRIES

80 to 100 maraschino cherries (with
    stems), drain on paper towels
1 (1/2-lb.) pkg. vanilla flavored candy
    coating (Plymouth Pantry or
    Eagle Brand)
1 T. Crisco shortening
1 tsp. almond flavoring

Melt coating for 90 seconds in microwave in glass microwaveable dish. Stir at 15 second intervals. Hold each cherry by stem and dip cherry into melted vanilla coating. Remove to wax paper-lined cookie sheets. Refrigerate. Remove from refrigerator 1/2 hour before serving. Serve on a lace paper doily lined silver or glass platter.

Beautiful and delicious!

Note: Chocolate flavored candy coating may be substituted. Recipe may be reduced in quantity according to how many cherries you need.

Teresa McCurry Tankersley
Lincolnton, GA

BUTTERSCOTCH FUDGE

2 1/4 C. granulated sugar
3/4 C. evaporated milk
1 C. marshmallow creme or
    16 lg. marshmallows
1/4 C. butter
1/4 tsp. salt
1 6-oz. pkg. butterscotch morsels
1 tsp. vanilla extract
1 C. coarsely chopped nuts

In a heavy saucepan, mix sugar, milk and marshmallow creme, butter and salt. Cook, stirring all the while over medium heat, until mixture comes to a boil. Boil and stir 5 minutes more. Remove from heat. Stir in butterscotch morsels. Melt completely. Add vanilla and nuts. Stir and spread in buttered 8" square pan. Cool and cut. Store in airtight container. Makes 30 pieces.

BUTTERMILK FUDGE

1/2 C. butter
1 C. buttermilk
2 T. white Karo syrup
1 tsp. baking soda
2 C. granulated sugar
1 C. chopped walnuts or pecans
1 T. vanilla

Place butter, buttermilk, syrup, soda and sugar in saucepan. Stir until sugar dissolves. Cook until soft ball stage (236°), using a candy thermometer. Remove from heat and cool to 110°. Beat until no longer glossy. Stir in nuts and vanilla. Pour immediately into buttered 8x8x2" pan and let get firm, but still warm, before slicing into squares. Makes 1 1/2 pounds.

HONEY FUDGE

2 squares unsweetened
    chocolate (2-oz.)
2 C. granulated sugar
1/8 tsp. salt
1 C. evaporated milk
1/4 C. honey
1 C. coarsely chopped nuts
2 T. butter

In a double boiler, melt chocolate over hot water. Add sugar, salt and milk and boil 5 minutes. Add honey and cook to soft ball stage (236°). Remove from heat. Cool to 110°, then add vanilla, nuts and butter. Beat until mixture is no longer glossy. When cool enough, knead on buttered surface a few times, then press into buttered 8x8x2" pan and let stand until firm. Cut into squares. Makes 1 1/2 pounds.

MARBLED FUDGE

2 C. granulated sugar
2/3 C. evaporated milk
1 C. whole milk
1/4 C. white Karo syrup
1/4 tsp. salt
1 tsp. vanilla
1/2 C. chopped semi-sweet
    chocolate morsels

In a heavy saucepan, combine sugar, milk, syrup and salt. Stir until sugar is dissolved. Boil and stir until candy thermometer is 238° or until a drop of mixture in cold water forms a soft ball. Remove from heat and cool 5 minutes. Beat in vanilla for about 5 minutes until thickened. Pour 1/2 of fudge in buttered 8x8x2" baking pan. Sprinkle with 1/2 of chocolate morsels. Pour in remaining 1/2 of fudge. Stir once, making one figure 8. Sprinkle with the remaining chocolate morsels. Cool until firm and cut into 1" cubes. Makes 1 1/4 pounds.

NANCY'S VELVEETA FUDGE

1 lb. butter
1 lb. Velveeta cheese
4 lb. confectioner's sugar
2 C. chopped nuts
1 C. cocoa

Melt cheese and butter; add sugar and nuts. Add cocoa last. Stir well. Pour into shallow baking dish. Let set until firm. Cut in small squares. Makes approximately 5 1/2 pounds.

Nancy Ferguson Blount
Lincolnton, GA

HAYSTACKS

3 8-oz. pkg. butterscotch morsels
1 lg. can Chinese noodles
2 C. dry roasted, salted peanuts

In the top of a double boiler over hot (not boiling) water, melt the butterscotch morsels. Mix the noodles and peanuts together in a large bowl and pour the melted butterscotch over it. Drop by heaping teaspoonfuls onto wax paper. Cool until firm and store in airtight containers.

PEANUT BRITTLE

2 C. granulated sugar
1 tsp. baking soda
2 C. raw peanuts
1 C. water
1 C. white Karo syrup

Combine sugar, syrup and water in an iron skillet and cook until boiling and mixture spins a thread (dip a little out, about 1 teaspoon, and pour back into skillet. If "thread" forms while pouring it's ready.) Add raw peanuts; cook until you hear peanuts stop popping, stirring constantly. Remove from heat; add soda; stir (will be foamy). Spread quickly on greased marble top or in greased baking sheets. Cool until firm; break into desired pieces. Store in an airtight container.

Be careful cooking this. Hot mixture will burn your fingers!

PEANUT BUTTER BALLS

1 1/2 C. graham cracker crumbs
1 1/3 C. peanut butter
1 lb. powdered sugar
1 1/2 sticks melted margarine
2/3 block paraffin
12 oz. chocolate chips

Combine first 4 ingredients and mix; shape into balls. Melt paraffin and chocolate chips in double boiler, and dip balls into chocolate mixture. Makes 100 balls.

LITTLE PECAN LOGS

1 7-oz. jar marshmallow creme
1 bx. powdered sugar
1 tsp. almond flavoring
1 pkg. Kraft caramels
1 T. milk
1 C. finely chopped pecans

Make the day before serving.
Combine the marshmallow creme, powdered sugar and flavoring. Mix well. Shape into "logs" (about 2/3 size of your little finger). Place on a flat plate; cover with plastic wrap and let stand overnight. Then melt caramels and milk in top of double boiler over water. Dip each "log" into caramels and roll in chopped nuts. Cool before serving.
Note: May be made into 2 large rolls and sliced. Use same procedure.

UNCOOKED CANDY

1 stick butter, melted
1 qt. pecans, chopped
1 14-oz. can sweetened
    condensed milk
1 can coconut
1/4 lb. paraffin
1 12-oz. pkg. semi-sweet
    chocolate morsels
2 1-lb. pkg. powdered sugar

Melt butter; pour over chopped pecans. Set aside. Mix sugar, coconut and milk. Add pecans. Shape into balls (about the size of a small walnut) and chill for 15 minutes. Melt chocolate and paraffin in the top of a double boiler over hot water. Using a toothpick or wooden skewer, dip each ball in the melted chocolate and drop on wax paper until cooled. Store in airtight container. Makes approximately 12 dozen.

WHITE TRASH

1/2 stick margarine
1 12-oz. pkg. chocolate chips
1 C. smooth peanut butter
1 12-oz. bx. Golden Graham cereal
1 bx. golden raisins
3 C. roasted, salted peanuts
1 bx. confectioner's sugar

In a large saucepan, melt butter, chocolate chips and peanut butter together. Fold in cereal, raisins and peanuts to coat. Pour box of sugar over mixture and with a fork in each hand, stir mixture gently to coat with sugar. Cool and store in airtight containers.

Sara Winn
Manchester, GA

- COOKIES -

BASIC NUT COOKIES

1 C. butter
1 1/2 C. confectioner's sugar, sifted
1 egg, beaten
1 tsp. vanilla
2 1/2 C. sifted plain flour
1 tsp. baking soda
1 tsp. cream of tartar
1/4 tsp. salt
1 C. finely chopped nuts (your choice)

Preheat oven to 350°. Combine butter and sugar; cream until fluffy. Fold in beaten egg and vanilla. Sift flour, baking soda, cream of tartar and salt. Blend thoroughly. Fold in nuts. Shape into balls (as big around as a quarter). Bake on an ungreased cookie sheet for 10 to 12 minutes. Cool.

Cookies freeze well.

CHOCOLATE CHIP COOKIES

2/3 C. soft shortening
1 1/2 C. flour
1/2 C. granulated sugar
1/2 tsp. soda
1/2 C. brown sugar, packed
1/2 tsp. salt
1 egg
1/2 C. chopped nuts (approx.)
1 tsp. vanilla
1 6-oz. pkg. chocolate chip pieces

Heat oven to 375°. Mix shortening, sugars, egg and vanilla thoroughly. Mix flour, soda and salt; blend in. Add chocolate chips and nuts. Drop 2" apart with teaspoon on ungreased baking sheet. Bake 8 to 10 minutes. Cool slightly before removing from sheet. Yield: 5 dozen.

Hal Radford
Lincolnton, GA

COCONUT MERINGUES

3 egg whites, stiffly beaten
3/4 C. sugar
1 tsp. almond extract
3/4 C. coconut, toasted

Preheat oven to 250°. Toast coconut in single layer on tray in toaster oven on light setting. Set aside. To stiffly beaten egg whites, add sugar gradually. Beat until very stiff; add almond extract and toasted coconut. Drop from 1/2 teaspoon measuring spoon onto wax paper-lined cookie sheet. Bake for 50 minutes. Store in airtight container. Makes 60 meringues.

FUDGE COOKIES

2 C. Minute oatmeal
1 tsp. vanilla
1 C. nuts or coconut
2 C. sugar
1/2 C. cocoa
1/2 C. milk
1 stick margarine

In a large bowl, mix oatmeal, vanilla and coconut. Combine sugar, cocoa, milk and margarine in a large saucepan; bring to a rolling boil. Pour boiling mixture over oatmeal mixture; stir thoroughly and drop by teaspoon on wax paper. Cool and eat!

Betty Miller Wilkins
Prosperity, SC

GOURMET GRAHAMS

20 whole graham crackers
2 1/2 sticks unsalted butter
1 1/2 C. packed light brown sugar
1/2 tsp. ground cinnamon
1 1/4 tsp. vanilla
2 C. coarsely chopped pecans, toasted
1 6-oz. pkg. semi-sweet chocolate
    morsels, slightly chopped

Place graham crackers in single layer with sides touching on 2 large buttered cookie sheets (with sides). Chop nuts and chocolate morsels; set aside. In a heavy saucepan, melt butter and add brown sugar. Stir over medium heat until smooth. Pour in cinnamon and vanilla. Boil 1½ minutes. Pour over graham crackers. Coat lightly with toasted pecans. Bake 8 to 10 minutes in preheated 350° oven. Remove from oven and top with chocolate morsels. Cool 3 or 4 minutes on cookie sheets. Cut around each cracker carefully and cool on a wire rack. When completely cooled, break or cut each graham cracker and store in an airtight container. Serve when cooled or the next day. Makes 40.
Delicious!

LACE PETTICOAT COOKIES

1 C. quick-cooking Quaker oats
    (uncooked)
1 C. granulated sugar
7 tsp. all-purpose flour (unsifted)
1/4 tsp. salt
1 lg. egg, beaten slightly
1/2 C. butter or margarine, melted
2 tsp. vanilla

In a mixing bowl, combine first 4 ingredients. Fold in remaining ingredients. Stir to blend. Line cookie sheets with aluminum foil. Drop cookie dough from 1/2 teaspoon measuring spoon onto lined cookie sheets. Bake at 350° for 6 to 8 minutes. Cool completely and store in an airtight container. Makes 6 dozen.

LYNDA'S LEMON COOKIES

1 bx. lemon supreme cake mix
4 oz. Cool Whip
1 egg, beaten

Mix together and roll into small balls. Roll in 4X powdered sugar. Place balls on cookie sheet. Bake at 350° for 10 minutes on top rack. Makes 7 dozen.

Lynda Rogers
Manchester, GA

OLD FASHIONED OATMEAL COOKIES

1 C. sifted all-purpose flour
3/4 tsp. soda
1/2 tsp. salt
1 tsp. cinnamon
1/4 tsp. nutmeg
3/4 C. shortening, soft
1 1/3 C. firmly packed brown sugar
2 eggs, beaten
1 tsp. vanilla
2 C. oats (uncooked)
1 C. raisins

Sift together flour, soda, salt, cinnamon and nutmeg into a bowl. Add shortening, sugar, eggs and vanilla; beat until smooth, about 2 minutes. Stir in oats and raisins. Drop by teaspoonfuls on greased cookie sheets. Bake at 350° for 15 minutes. Yield: 3 1/2 dozen.

GRANNIE'S PEANUT BUTTER COOKIES

3 C. plain flour
2 tsp. soda
1/4 tsp. salt
1 C. shortening
1 C. granulated sugar
1 C. brown sugar
2 eggs
1 C. peanut butter
1 tsp. vanilla

Sift flour once before measuring, then sift again with soda and salt. Cream shortening, granulated sugar and brown sugar. Add beaten eggs and mix until smooth. Add peanut butter; stir well, then add flour mixture. Mix to a stiff batter and add vanilla. Form into tiny balls with palms of hands and press onto greased cookie sheet. Press with back of fork to make waffle design. Sprinkle with sugar. Bake for 15 minutes. If desired, dough may be rolled, placed in refrigerator for several hours, then sliced. Makes about 4 dozen small cookies.

Beth's favorite.

Grace Booker Radford
Dawson, GA

PEANUT BUTTER CHIP COOKIES

1 C. shortening or 3/4 C. butter or
   margarine
1 C. sugar
1/2 C. packed light brown sugar
1 tsp. vanilla
2 eggs
2 C. unsifted all-purpose flour
1 tsp. baking soda
2 C. (12-oz. pkg.) Reese's
   peanut butter chips

Cream shortening or butter or margarine, sugar, brown sugar and vanilla until light and fluffy. Add eggs and beat well. Combine flour and baking soda; add to creamed mixture. Stir in peanut butter chips. Drop by teaspoonfuls onto ungreased cookie sheet. Bake at 350° for 10 to 12 minutes or until light brown. Cool slightly before removing from cookie sheet. Makes about 5 dozen 2 1/2" cookies.

PEANUT BUTTER KISSES

1 lg. egg, beaten
1 C. crunchy peanut butter
1 C. granulated sugar
36 unwrapped Hershey's
   kisses with almonds

Combine beaten egg, peanut butter and sugar. Make into 36 (3/4") balls. Bake on ungreased cookie sheet. Remove from oven and immediately place a "kiss" in center of each, pressing down gently. Bake at 350° for 12 minutes. Cool on cookie sheet 5 minutes, then remove to wire rack carefully to cool completely. Store in airtight container. Make 3 dozen.

PECAN DROPS

1 egg white
1 C. brown sugar
1 1/4 C. chopped pecans
1 1/2 T. flour

Lightly grease cookie sheets. Beat egg white until frothy; add sugar a little at a time, beating well after each addition. Beat with electric mixer until stiff peaks form. Fold in pecans and flour. Using a teaspoonful of mixture for each cookie, shape mixture into ball and place 2" apart on cookie sheet. Bake at 350° for 10 minutes. Store in airtight container. Makes approximately 2 1/2 to 3 dozen.

PECAN MERINGUES

2 eggs whites, beaten stiff
1/2 C. sugar
1 tsp. vanilla extract
1/2 C. pecans*, ground or
    very finely chopped

*Walnuts or almonds may also be used.

To stiffly beaten egg whites, add sugar, a little at a time. Continue beating until very stiff, then add vanilla and gently fold in nuts. Place on wax paper-lined cookie sheet by using 1/2 teaspoon measuring spoon. Bake in preheated 250° oven for 50 minutes. Makes 48 (very small) meringues.

POTATO CHIP COOKIES

1 C. Crisco shortening
1 C. light brown sugar
1 C. granulated sugar
2 beaten eggs
2 C. all-purpose flour
1 tsp. soda
2 C. crushed potato chips
1 6-oz. pkg. butterscotch bits
1 tsp. vanilla extract

In a large bowl, combine Crisco and sugars; cream well. Add eggs. Sift flour and soda together. Add to egg mixture. Add potato chips, butterscotch bits and vanilla. Drop by level teaspoonfuls onto ungreased cookie sheets. Bake in a preheated 325° oven for 10 to 12 minutes. Cool slightly, remove from cookie sheets and place on paper towels to finish cooling; then store in airtight container.

No one can guess that potato chips are in them and they are delicious!

SHORTIN' BREAD

4 C. all-purpose flour
1 C. light brown sugar, packed
1 lb. butter, melted

Sift flour and sugar together. Add melted butter; mix until smooth dough forms. Place dough on floured surface. Press down gently until 1/2" thick. Cut with small cookie cutter in shapes desired. Bake at 325° for 20 to 25 minutes. Makes 50 cookies.

This recipe is as old as the South!

SUGAR COOKIES

1 C. sugar
1/3 C. butter
1 egg
1/3 C. buttermilk
1/3 tsp. soda
1 tsp. vanilla
Plain flour

Cream butter, sugar and egg. Add soda to buttermilk and stir. Add vanilla and flour enough to hold together a firm dough. Turn on floured surface; knead; cut when rolled very thin. Sprinkle with sugar. Bake at 350° for 10 to 12 minutes. Makes approximately 100 cookies.

Good for cut-out cookies all year long.

OLD FASHIONED TEA CAKES

1 C. sugar
1/2 C. margarine
1 egg, beaten
1 tsp. vanilla
2 C. sifted self-rising flour
Sugar

Cream 1 cup sugar and margarine. Add beaten egg and vanilla. Mix. Add flour. Knead until the consistency of biscuit dough. Place small balls of dough on an ungreased cookie sheet and flatten with a fork. Sprinkle top with sugar. Bake at 350° for 10 minutes. Makes 4 dozen.

Lynda Rogers
Manchester, GA

VANILLA SUGAR

3 vanilla beans, broken
   into 2" long pieces
1 lb. powdered sugar, sifted

Combine ingredients. Let stand for 3 days. Use in coffee or cookie recipes.

- BROWNIES -

CHOCOLATE CHIP BROWNIES

2/3 C. melted margarine
2 C. brown sugar
2 eggs
2 tsp. vanilla
2 C. flour
1 tsp. baking powder
1 tsp. soda
1/4 tsp. salt
1 6-oz. pkg. chocolate chips

Mix margarine, brown sugar, vanilla, and eggs. Add flour, salt, baking powder and soda. Stir in chocolate chips. Pour into large greased 9x13" cake pan. Bake at 350° for 30 to 40 minutes.

QUICK AND EASY BROWNIES

1 stick margarine
1 C. granulated sugar
4 eggs
1 can Hershey chocolate syrup
1 C. all-purpose flour
3/4 C. chopped nuts

In a mixing bowl, cream margarine and sugar together. Add eggs, one at a time, beating after each. Pour in syrup. Stir. Add flour a little at a time (in fourths). Fold in nuts. Pour into greased 15x12" jelly-roll pan or cookie sheet with sides. Bake at 350° for 25 minutes. Cut when cooled.

4 squares unsweetened chocolate
1 1/2 sticks butter
2 C. granulated sugar
3 eggs, beaten
1 tsp. vanilla
1 C. all-purpose flour
1 1/2 C. chopped nuts

In a heavy saucepan, melt chocolate and butter together, stirring often until smooth and chocolate has melted completely. Remove from heat. Mix in sugar until blended, then add eggs and vanilla. Stir in flour and nuts. Place in a buttered 13x9" baking pan. Bake in preheated 350° oven for 30 to 35 minutes. Cool. Cut into desired number of squares.

Great for a tailgate picnic!

Note: Spraying the pan with Baker's Joy works wonders!

Desserts

- DESSERTS -

APPLE CRISP

6 C. sliced apples
1/4 tsp. cinnamon
1 C. flour
2 C. sugar
1 stick margarine, melted
1 egg

Place sliced apples in baking dish. Mix 1 cup sugar with 1/4 teaspoon cinnamon and spread over apples. Mix 1 cup flour, 1 cup sugar and 1 egg. Stir until crumbly. Spread over apples. Drizzle melted butter over all. Bake at 300° for 45 minutes until brown.

APPLE DESSERT

6 apples, peeled, cored and
    sliced 1/4" thick
2 T. lemon juice
1/4 C. seedless raisins
1/2 C. sugar
1/2 tsp. ground cinnamon
20 lg. marshmallows

Place sliced apples in a buttered baking dish. Stir in lemon juice. Stir in raisins. Mix the cinnamon and sugar together. Sprinkle over top. Bake covered until apples are tender. Uncover, top with marshmallows and bake until brown and puffy at 350°. Serve hot.
Note: 3/4 cup chopped nuts may be added.

TOUARD APPLE CHEESE DESSERT

1 stick butter or margarine
1 C. granulated sugar
1/4 lb. Velveeta cheese
3/4 C. self-rising flour
1 20-oz. can Thank You brand apples
    (label has green Granny Smith
    apples), without sugar

Butter a 9x13" casserole dish. Pour in apples (do not drain). In microwave, melt butter, sugar and cheese. Add flour to butter mixture. Pour over apples and bake at 350° for 20 to 25 minutes. Serve hot.
Good with a scoop of vanilla ice cream on each serving.

Brenda Touard
Chapin, SC

FROZEN BANANAS

Bananas (1 per serving)
Sugar (granulated)
Whipping cream (1/2 pt. for
    4 to 6 bananas), chilled
Cherries (with stems)
Sliced almonds (optional)

Peel bananas; wrap each one in Saran wrap and freeze. Just before serving, slice frozen bananas in dessert dishes. Sprinkle with sugar. Pour chilled whipping cream (enough to coat bananas). The cream will freeze to the banana slices. Sprinkle a few almonds over the bananas and top with a stemmed cherry.

Easy and unusual!

CHEESECAKE (EASY)

Crust:
2 C. graham cracker crumbs,
    or 2 C. gingersnap crumbs
1/2 C. sugar
1/2 C. melted butter

Combine graham cracker crumbs, sugar and melted butter. Pat into a springform pan or a 2-quart baking dish.

Filling:
2 8-oz. pkg. cream cheese, softened
2 eggs
2/3 C. sugar

Beat softened cream cheese, eggs and sugar together until smooth. Pour into crumb Crust and gently pat until level. Bake at 375° for 20 minutes. Take out of oven; cool 15 minutes. Meanwhile, increase oven temperature to 425°.

Topping:
1 C. sour cream
2 T. sugar
1 tsp. vanilla

Mix sour cream, sugar and vanilla. Spread on top of Cheesecake and immediately return to oven and bake for 10 more minutes. Remove from oven and refrigerate overnight. Freezes well, too.

CHOCOLATE ICEBOX DESSERT

1 angel food cake (partially frozen)
6 eggs, separated
1 12-oz. bag semi-sweet
   chocolate chips
4 T. sugar
6 T. water
2 tsp. vanilla
1 tsp. salt
2 C. whipping cream

Line a 9x9" cake pan with wax paper. Slice partially frozen cake and place one layer of slices. Beat egg yolks. Reserve whites. Melt chocolate chips in a double boiler over hot water; add sugar and water. Mix well until chocolate and sugar are melted. Remove from heat. Gradually stir chocolate mixture into beaten egg yolks. Beat until smooth. Cool. Add vanilla and salt; mix. Beat egg whites until stiff; whip cream. Fold egg whites and whipped cream into cooled chocolate mixture. Pour chocolate mixture over first layer of angel food cake; then alternate chocolate mixture and cake slices with chocolate last. Chill overnight.

NANNIE'S CHOCOLATE DELIGHT

Crust:
1 1/4 C. flour
1/2 C. chopped walnuts
1 cube soft butter

Mix and put into bottom of a 9x13" pan. Bake for 20 minutes at 350°. Cool completely.

Filling:
8 oz. cream cheese (real soft)
1 C. powdered sugar
1/2 lg. ctn. Cool Whip

Mix and spread on top of Crust

Topping:
2 sm. pkg. instant chocolate pudding
3 C. milk
1/2 lg. ctn. Cool Whip
Nuts, toasted

Mix chocolate pudding and milk together and spread on Filling. Top with other 1/2 of Cool Whip. Sprinkle with nuts. Keep refrigerated until served. Slice into squares. Serve on chilled glass dessert plates.

This was Nannie's favorite dessert.

Mattie Maude McCurry
(Mother of the Twelve)
Lincolnton, GA

DATE NUT ROLL

2 C. vanilla wafer crumbs
1 C. chopped dates
1/2 C. chopped nuts
1/2 C. sweetened condensed milk
2 tsp. lemon juice

Mix milk with lemon juice. Set aside. Combine crumbs, dates and pecans in a mixing bowl. Add milk mixture. Knead well and shape into a 3" roll. Wrap in plastic wrap and refrigerate for 12 hours. Slice. Serve with whipped cream.

FRUIT DELIGHT

2 C. flour
3/4 C. vegetable oil
1/4 C. water
1 tsp. vanilla
1 8-oz. pkg. cream cheese, softened
1 (4 1/2-oz.) ctn. Cool Whip, thawed
1 bx. 4X confectioner's sugar
1 can blueberry pie filling
1/2 C. chopped pecans

Mix flour, vegetable oil, water and vanilla. Spread in 9x13" buttered baking dish. Bake at 350° until brown. Cool.

In the meantime, mix softened cream cheese, thawed Cool Whip and sugar. Spread over cooled "crust". Top with blueberry pie filling (or any pie filling of your choice). Sprinkle chopped pecans on top. Serves approximately 15.

LUSCIOUS LEMON SQUARES

2 C. plain flour, sifted
1/2 C. 10X powdered sugar
2 sticks melted butter
6 T. lemon juice
2 C. sugar
4 T. plain flour
4 eggs, beaten until slightly frothy
    and yellow and color
1/2 tsp. baking powder

Mix first 3 ingredients together and place in a 12x9" baking dish. Bake for 20 minutes at 350°. Remove from oven. Mix last 5 ingredients. Pour over baked layer. Bake again for 25 minutes. Remove from oven. Cool slightly and dust with powdered sugar. Cut in small squares. Cool. Store in airtight container.

MERINGUE SHELLS

12 egg whites, beaten until stiff
2 1/2 C. granulated sugar
2 tsp. vanilla extract

To stiffly beaten egg whites, very gradually add sugar (about 1 tablespoon at a time), beating all the while. Add vanilla last. Put a sheet of wax paper on a cookie sheet. If you are making small shells, drop the meringue onto the paper by tablespoonfuls and make a little hollow (to hold filling) in the center with the back of the spoon. For large shells, use 2 table-spoons of meringue and make hollow in the middle. Bake for 45 minutes at 250°, then turn oven off and leave meringues in oven for 30 more minutes. Store in airtight container. Makes 48 small or 24 large meringues.

To crisp before serving, you may reheat them for 10 minutes at 155°. Fill with choice of fillings.

GEORGIA FRIED PEACHES

1 can peach halves, drained
3 T. butter
1/4 C. peach schnapps (optional)
Brown sugar
Vanilla or peach ice cream or
    whipped cream

Melt butter in heavy skillet. Place drained peaches, rounded side down, into skillet. Fill each hollow with brown sugar. Pour schnapps over sugar. Cook on medium heat until top of peach is warm to touch and brown sugar has begun to melt. Remove from skillet to dessert plate and top each peach half with a scoop of ice cream or whipped cream. Makes 6 to 8 servings.

PECAN ROLLS

Biscuit dough
3/4 C. butter or margarine
2 C. brown sugar
3/4 C. coarsely chopped pecans

Make a recipe of your favorite biscuit dough. Cream butter and sugar. Place in a saucepan over medium heat and melt. Add pecans. Spread 1/2 of mixture on dough which has been rolled out to 1/2" thick by 5" wide oblong piece. Roll up as you would a jelly-roll. Cut in 3/4" slices. Spread remaining filling in bottom of round cake pan. Put rolls in single layer on top of this and bake at 375° for 25 to 30 minutes. Remove carefully. Serve with bottom mixture on top.

BAKED PINEAPPLE DESSERT

1 C. flour
1 C. brown sugar
1 tsp. soda
1/2 tsp. salt
1 egg
1 (8 1/2-oz.) can crushed pineapple

In a mixing bowl, mix flour, brown sugar, soda, salt, beaten egg and crushed pineapple. Pour into a greased 8x10" baking dish. Sprinkle Topping over. Bake at 350° for 30 to 40 minutes. Serve with whipped cream. Makes approximately 8 servings.

Topping:
1/4 C. brown sugar
1/4 C. chopped pecans

Mix ingredients.

PINEAPPLE REFRIGERATOR CAKE

1 14-oz. can sweetened
   condensed milk
1 C. crushed pineapple, well drained
3 T. lemon juice
3 C. vanilla wafer crumbs, crushed fine
1/2 C. chopped nuts

Combine lemon juice and condensed milk. When thickened, add well-drained pineapple and nuts. Line a Pyrex dish with wax paper. Beginning with a layer of crumbs, place alternating layers of crumbs and pineapple mixture until all ingredients are used. Refrigerate overnight. Slice and serve with whipped cream and a cherry if you like. Makes 12 servings.

POPPY SEED TART SHELLS

1 C. all-purpose flour (unsifted), chilled
2 tsp. granulated sugar
1 tsp. poppy seeds
1/4 tsp. salt
6 T. butter or margarine (cold)
2 to 3 T. very cold water

In a mixing bowl, combine chilled flour, sugar, poppy seeds and salt. Cut in butter until mixture is like coarse crumbs. Stir in water, 1 tablespoon at a time. When mixture holds together, form into 4 equal balls. Roll each ball on a floured surface to 5" circles and place each one in a 4" tart pan (preferably one with a removable bottom). Trim around edges. Pierce bottom and sides with a fork. Bake in preheated 400° oven for 15 to 20 minutes. Cool on a wire rack. Fill as desired.

SHORTCAKE DOUGH

2 C. sifted plain flour
2 tsp. baking powder
3/4 tsp. salt
1/2 C. shortening (Crisco)
3/4 C. buttermilk

Sift dry ingredients into large mixing bowl. Cut in shortening with pastry cutter. Slowly stir in milk with knife until a soft dough forms. Turn dough onto floured surface. Flour hands and toss lightly from hand to hand a few times; return to floured surface and knead a few strokes. Roll or pat out 3/4" thick. Bake at 450° for 15 minutes. Split in half and fill. Makes 16 (2") biscuits.

Cut 3/4" thick; cut into rounds or pat out and cut in squares with a knife.

STRAWBERRY REFRIGERATOR CAKES

1 sm. pkg. strawberry Jell-O
1 C. water
1 C. sugar
1 pt. frozen strawberries
1 14-oz. can sweetened
    condensed milk, chilled
2 T. lemon juice
1 9-oz. pkg. vanilla wafers

Using a hand mixer, whip lemon juice and chilled milk together. In a saucepan, mix Jell-O, water and sugar; heat and mix with strawberries. Fold mixture into whipped milk. Line an 8x11x2" dish with wax paper. Beginning with a layer of vanilla wafers, alternate layers of wafers and milk/strawberry mixture. Place in freezer until firm. Cut into squares and serve. Top with whipped cream and fresh strawberries.

- FROZEN DESSERTS -

ELEGANT CHOCOLATE DESSERT

1/2 C. butter or margarine
1 C. sifted powdered sugar
2 squares melted bitter chocolate
2 eggs
1 1/2 tsp. vanilla
Whipped cream and crushed pecans,
    for garnish

Mix butter and sugar in electric mixer until fluffy. Add chocolate, beating constantly; add eggs, beating constantly, then add vanilla. Pour into 4 dessert dishes; cover with wax paper and freeze. When ready to serve, remove from freezer, top with whipped cream and crushed pecans. Since it does not freeze hard, there is no need to thaw the dessert before serving.

ORANGE ICE

2 oranges
4 C. water
2 1/2 C. sugar
2 C. orange juice
1/2 C. lemon juice

Peel the rind as thinly as possible from the oranges; place rinds of oranges in a saucepan with water and sugar. Cook on medium heat for 20 minutes. Remove rind and seeds; add fruit juices; pour through strainer; cool and freeze in a shallow dish. Serve in stemmed or parfait glasses. Garnish with whipped cream and a cherry and/or a few strips of lemon zest*. Makes 6 to 8 servings.

*Zest is made by peeling very thin strips from orange rind with a vegetable parer or a "zester".

CAROLINA PEACH ICE CREAM

12 fresh peaches, peeled and sliced
2 C. sugar
1 14-oz. can sweetened
   condensed milk
2 qt. milk
1 8-oz. ctn. sour cream
2 tsp. vanilla

Mix peaches and sugar together in a blender. Add to other ingredients. Churn until frozen. Makes 4 quarts.

GEORGIA PEACH ICE CREAM

2 cans sweetened condensed milk
4 C. fresh peaches,
   peeled and mashed
1 T. flour
1 T. vanilla
2 qt. whole milk

In a large bowl, combine condensed milk, peaches and flour. Beat well. Add vanilla and remaining milk. Mix well. Pour into freezer can of ice cream churn and freeze. Use hand or electric churn. Follow churn directions to freeze. Makes 1 gallon.

PRALINE ICE CREAM SQUARES

Crust:
2 C. plain flour
3/4 C. uncooked oatmeal
1 C. melted margarine
1 C. chopped pecans
1/2 C. light brown sugar

Preheat oven to 400°. Combine in order listed and crumble on a cookie sheet. Bake for 15 to 20 minutes; stir during baking time to brown evenly. Press half the mixture into a 9x13" pan (disposable aluminum pans are perfect).

Filling:
2 (1/2-gal.) ctn. vanilla ice cream (rectangular ctn.)
1 12-oz. jar caramel sauce
1 C. chopped pecans, toasted

Slice 1 1/2 to 2" thick slices of ice cream and place on top of Crust. Pour caramel sauce and toasted pecans over top of ice cream. Top with remaining crust (crumbled). Cover with foil or plastic wrap and freeze 4 to 6 hours. Cut in squares. Serve on chilled dessert plates. Makes 16 to 18 servings.

Note: Put dry dessert plates in a stack in freezer to chill.

SOUTHERN SNOWBALLS

1 qt. vanilla ice cream
1 7-oz. can shredded coconut

Roll ice cream into 2" balls. Roll in coconut. Freeze in single layer on a wax paper lined cookie sheet.

Praline Sauce:
1/2 C. cream
1 lb. caramels

Heat in double boiler until smooth. Serve hot over "snowballs".

- PUDDINGS -

UNCLE BOBBY'S BANANA PUDDING (FROM SCRATCH)

1 1/2 C. granulated sugar
2 C. whole milk
4 lg. eggs
2 T. plain flour
Pinch of salt
Pinch of baking powder
2 tsp. vanilla
6 to 8 bananas, peeled and sliced
1 16-oz. bx. vanilla wafers

Mix flour, sugar, salt and baking powder. Add milk; mix well. Beat eggs and add to other mixture. Add vanilla; mix well. Cook in a double boiler over boiling water until thick. Line a large casserole dish with vanilla wafers. Cover with a layer of bananas, then a layer of pudding. Repeat layers until all ingredients are used. Cover top with a layer of vanilla wafers.

Note: If you wish to top with meringue, beat 3 egg whites until stiff peaks form; add 1/3 cup sugar and 1 teaspoon cornstarch. Beat until stiff and spread on top. Bake at 350° until lightly brown.

Uncle Bobby has bananas growing in his back yard. He really does make this "from scratch".

Bobby McCurry
(One of the Twelve)
St. Petersburg, FL

BLUEBERRY PUDDING

1 egg, slightly beaten
1 1/2 C. flour, sifted
2 tsp. baking powder
5 T. shortening
1/4 C. sugar
1/2 tsp. salt
3/4 C. milk*
1 C. blueberries, washed and drained
    (fresh, frozen or canned)

*Or more -- enough to make a dough that is stiffer than cake dough.

Mix dry ingredients; cut in shortening as for biscuit dough. Add milk and beaten egg. Stir until smooth. Add blueberries. Stir slightly and bake in an 8x8" baking pan at 350° for 30 minutes. Serve warm. Makes 8 servings.

Very good with Caramel Sauce (see Table of Contents).

OLD FASHIONED BREAD PUDDING

2 eggs, beaten
2 C. milk
1/2 C. granulated sugar
1/2 tsp. ground nutmeg
1/2 tsp. ground cinnamon
4 C. dry bread or cake, cut in cubes
1/3 C. raisins
1/3 C. finely chopped nuts
1/4 tsp. vanilla

In a mixing bowl, beat eggs, milk and sugar together until smooth. Add nutmeg and cinnamon. Place bread or cake cubes in a baking dish. Pour egg mixture over this and let stand until cubes are soaked. Stir in raisins, nuts and vanilla. Bake at 350° for 20 minutes. Serve warm with sauce of your choice. (See Sauce section for recipe).

TIPSY PUDDING

1 9-oz. bx. vanilla wafers, crushed fine
1 stick butter, softened
1 C. sugar
1/3 C. bourbon
4 eggs
2 C. coarsely chopped pecans, toasted
1/2 tsp. vanilla
Whipped cream

In a double boiler, cream butter and sugar together. Add eggs, one at a time, beating slightly. Cook until thickened. Slowly add bourbon. Stir until smooth. Cool. Put in a 9x13" glass dish in layers. Wafers first, then pudding, then nuts; repeat. Finish with wafers on top. Serve in fancy sherbet glasses. Top with whipped cream and a stemmed red cherry. Makes 6 to 8 servings.

- FILLINGS & SAUCES -

LEMON FILLING FOR TARTS OR MERINGUES

5 eggs, beaten until lemon colored
2 C. granulated sugar
10 T. unsalted butter, melted
1/2 C. grated lemon rind
2/3 C. fresh lemon juice

In a large mixing bowl, beat eggs until thick and yellow; add sugar gradually. Pour melted butter in slowly in a small stream, beating constantly. Pour in lemon rind and juice until blended. Pour mixture into top of double boiler over very hot (not boiling) water. Cook 10 minutes until thick, stirring all the while. Cool. Store in covered glass jars in refrigerator until ready to use. Make 3 3/4 cups.

Use to fill individual tarts, cakes or just give a jar as a gift.

BUTTERSCOTCH SAUCE

4 T. butter
1 C. brown sugar, packed
1 tsp. cornstarch
1/2 tsp. vinegar
1/4 C. water

In a heavy saucepan, combine all ingredients. Bring to a boil and cook until thickened. Serve hot. Makes approximately 3/4 cup.

CARAMEL SAUCE

1 C. packed brown sugar
1/2 pt. whipping cream
1 C. Half and Half
3 T. butter

Combine all ingredients in top of double boiler over hot water. Cook slowly for 2 hours. Stir occasionally. Serve hot, over cake or ice cream. Makes approximately 8 servings.

CHOCOLATE MARSHMALLOW SAUCE

8 oz. marshmallows, cut in pieces
4 oz. semi-sweet chocolate morsels
1/2 C. hot milk or cream

In the top of a double boiler, over boiling water, place marshmallows, chocolate and cream. Cook over medium-high heat, stirring constantly, until smooth. Serve hot. Makes approximately 1 1/4 cups.

Good over ice cream.

LEMON SAUCE

1 C. granulated sugar
2 T. cornstarch
2 C. boiling water
1 lemon (rind grated and
    juice of lemon)
2 T. butter

Stir the sugar and cornstarch together; slowly add boiling water, stirring all the while. Cook 7 to 10 minutes. Add grated lemon rind, juice and butter. Serve hot or cold over cake or pudding. Makes approximately 2 cups.

MINTED FRUIT SAUCE

6 stems of mint, stems and leaves
1 C. hot water
1/2 C. sugar
1/8 tsp. salt
1 1/2 tsp. cornstarch

Combine all ingredients in food processor or blender for 10 to 15 seconds. Pour into a saucepan; cook over low heat, stirring all the while, until mixture is thick and fairly transparent. Cool and use as a sauce for any fresh or canned fruit. Makes 6 to 8 servings.

Very pretty over melon balls in sherbet or parfait glasses.

ORDER FORM
Hospitality Southern Style

(Southern Recipes Cookbook)

Make checks payable to:
Heirlooms by Radford

Mail to:
Heirlooms by Radford
P. O. Box 517
Lincolnton, GA 30817

Name _____

Address _____

City _____ State _____ Zip _____

Please send .... copy(ies) of HOSPITALITY SOUTHERN STYLE cookbook at $17.95 plus $2.00 postage and handling each (Ga residents add sales tax). Enclosed is my check or money order in the amount of $ ....

For WHOLESALE rates, call 1-800-858-1062.

ORDER FORM
. . . hearts go home for the holidays

(Holiday Recipes Cookbook)

Make checks payable to:
Heirlooms by Radford

Mail to:
Heirlooms by Radford
P. O. Box 517
Lincolnton, GA 30817

Name _____

Address _____

City _____ State _____ Zip _____

Please send .... copy(ies) of . . . HEARTS GO HOME FOR THE HOLIDAYS cookbook at $17.95 plus $2.00 postage and handling each (Ga residents add sales tax). Enclosed is my check or money order in the amount of $ ....

For WHOLESALE rates, call 1-800-858-1062.

NOTES